Praise for
# SORRY, NO ENGLISH

"This book is a great idea and fills a real need that we have every day. With a largely diverse population in our local government setting, making this book available to our staff would be a game changer."

Corinne Sandefer
Director of Training
Loudoun County, Virginia

"There is such a great need for this book due to the increasing diversity in today's society. Given Storti's experience, both with ESL teaching and with intercultural training, he is uniquely qualified to write a book that not only addresses the language itself but also the nuanced cultural contexts around the use of language."

Darla Deardorff
Director, Association of Intl. Education Administrators
Founding President, World Council on
Intercultural and Global Competence

"According to Census Bureau data from 2018, over 20% of the US population speaks a language other than English at home. While many US citizens are bilingual, many are not or may even be monolingual. Craig Storti's book *Sorry, No English* meets a crucial need, with 50 easy-to-use suggestions on how native speakers can minimize communication challenges for limited-English speakers and improve information exchange."

Dr. Suzanne Panferov-Reese<br>
Past president of TESOL

"As an English language educator and someone who has been immersed in another language and culture for more than 20 years, this is an absolute must-read. These valuable tips not only serve as a guide for those in public-facing positions, but for those in education, like me, who work daily with others from the international community. I wish I would have read this twenty years ago when I first began my career in language education."

James L. Hensley M.S.Ed., TEFL/TESL<br>
Professor of English Language Education<br>
Joint Forces Military University<br>
Korea Defense Language Institute<br>
Icheon, South Korea

Craig Storti is available as a trainer/consultant in the subjects covered in this book. He can be reached at:

Email: craig@craigstorti.com

Website: craigstorti.com

Craig Storti is also the author of:

- *Americans at Work: A Guide to the Can-Do People*
- *The Art of Coming Home*
- *The Art of Crossing Cultures*
- *The Art of Doing Business Across Cultures*
- *Cross-Cultural Dialogues: 74 Brief Encounters with Cultural Difference*
  *(2nd edition)*
- *Speaking of India*
- *The Hunt for Mount Everest*
- *Incident at Bitter Creek*
- *Old World/New World—Bridging Cultural Differences: Britain, France, Germany and the U.S.*
- *Why Travel Matters*
- *Understanding the World's Cultures*

# SORRY, NO ENGLISH

## 50 TIPS TO IMPROVE YOUR COMMUNICATION WITH SPEAKERS OF LIMITED ENGLISH

CRAIG STORTI

**Chambers**

First published in Great Britain and the United States by Chambers in 2022
An imprint of John Murray Press
A division of Hodder & Stoughton Ltd
An Hachette UK company

28 27 26 25 24 23 22 1 2 3 4 5 6 7 8 9 10

Library of Congress Control Number: 2022931578
A CIP catalogue record for this title is available from the British Library

Paperback ISBN 978 1 529 39688 1
eBook ISBN 978 1 529 39689 8

John Murray Press policy is to use papers that are natural, renewable and recyclable products and made from wood grown in sustainable forests. The logging and manufacturing processes are expected to conform to the environmental regulations of the country of origin.

John Murray Press
Carmelite House
50 Victoria Embankment
London EC4Y 0DZ
www.chambers.co.uk

# TABLE OF CONTENTS

*Oh, the rare happiness of comprehending every single word that is said, and knowing that every word one says in return will be understood as well.*

—Mark Twain
*The Innocents Abroad*

# ACKNOWLEDGMENTS

Just as books don't write themselves—although this particular one was unusually painless—they also don't produce themselves. I am very grateful to all the folks at Hachette, both in North America and in the UK, who turned my manuscript into such a classy book. Sarah Cole made some excellent content suggestions very early on which added great value, and she was always there after that to help at every step along the way. Michelle Surianello was likewise a stalwart throughout the entire production process, and Melissa Carl will doubtless work her usual magic when it comes to sales and marketing. I'd also like to thank the copyeditor, Lisa Hutchins, for her close reading and countless suggestions.

The business of writing books all started for me some 30 years and 10 books ago with Intercultural Press and the late David Hoopes. The press was sold to Nicholas Brealey which eventually became a part of HBG. All along the way I have always been treated with the greatest courtesy, respect, and professionalism by folks like those mentioned above and by numerous others singled out in my previous acknowledgments. I don't know what it is like for authors who work with other publishers, but I have no particular desire to find out. The treatment I receive from the folks at HBG suits me just fine.

Craig Storti
Westminster, Maryland
Spring, 2022

# INTRODUCTION

Imagine this scene: You work at the reception desk in an office that offers free prenatal care to low-income pregnant women. Mrs. Garcia has come in this morning to register for the office's service, and you speak to her as follows:

You:            Good morning, Mrs. Garcia. What brings you here today?

Mrs. Garcia:    Excuse me?

You:            How can I help you?

Mrs. Garcia:    I need your service.

You:            Of course. Here are some forms for you to fill out. We'll also need to verify your income.

Mrs. Garcia:    Yes.

You:            The doctor's running behind this morning, but I'll try to squeeze you in. Sorry for all the red tape, but you'll get through it. Just bring the forms back to me when you're finished.

Mrs. Garcia:    Yes.

You:            Do you have any questions?

Mrs. Garcia:    No. Thank you.

In this brief exchange, you have made a total of 12 "mistakes," 12 things you said that Mrs. Garcia might not have understood.

Here's another scene: You work at the circulation desk of the local library and Mrs. Tran has come in to apply for a library card, with her two children:

| | |
|---|---|
| Mrs. Tran: | I would like to apply for a library card. |
| You: | Of course. Do you reside in the county? |
| Mrs. Tran: | Which side of the county? |
| You: | I mean. Where is your residence? |
| Mrs. Tran: | Yes, we are residents. |
| You: | Where is your house? |
| Mrs. Tran: | Oh, I see. In Rosslyn. |
| You: | Fine. Here is an application form. Please complete it and bring it back to me. |

### LATER...

| | |
|---|---|
| Mrs. Tran: | Here is my application. |
| You: | Thank you. Did you want this application to also cover your kids? |
| Mrs. Tran: | My kids? |
| You: | Yes. Your children? |
| Mrs. Tran: | Yes, please. |
| You: | You can borrow up to six books at once and two DVDs and hold on to them for three weeks. |
| Mrs. Tran: | Thank you. |
| You: | But if the books are late, there will be a fine. |

| Mrs. Tran: | It's fine if the books are late? |
| You: | No. You will have to pay. But if we are closed when you come back, there is always the book drop outside. |
| Mrs. Tran: | We can drop the books outside? |

Depending on how you count them, there are as many as eight possible "difficulties" for Mrs. Tran in this exchange.

Here's a scene in a restaurant where a limited-English couple is being waited on by their friendly server Jason. How many "difficult" things does Jason say?

| Jason: | Good evening. My name is Jason. I'll be your server this evening. What can I start you off with? |
| Patrons: | Excuse me? |
| Jason: | Can I get you something to drink? |
| Patrons: | Oh, yes. We'd like.... |
| Jason: | Sure. Let me grab those for you while you look over the menu. |

### LATER...

| Jason: | So, here are your drinks. We have several specials tonight. Can I go over them for you? |
| Patrons: | Yes, it's a very special night. |
| Jason: | No, I mean some dishes that are not on the menu. |
| Patrons: | Oh, then we can't have those tonight? |
| Jason: | No, I mean they're not written on the menu. |

Patrons:     Oh, of course.

### (JASON DESCRIBES THE SPECIALS.)

Jason:      I'll give you a few minutes.

### LATER...

Jason:      So, have we made up our minds?
Patrons:    Excuse me?
Jason:      I mean can I take your orders?
Patrons:    Our orders?

If you're a typical native speaker of English, you probably won't be able to identify many of the "mistakes" the speakers made in these three scenes. If that is true, and if you also work in a public-facing job, then there's a very good chance you could make mistakes just like these on a regular basis, not to mention numerous others we will describe in these pages.

Granted, these aren't mistakes in the sense of incorrect or ungrammatical English. They are mistakes, rather, in the sense that Mrs. Garcia, Mrs. Tran, and our restaurant couple will not understand what you/Jason are telling them, and they may not be able to complete their business with you today. And you will not have succeeded in doing your job.

If all that is okay with you, then you've picked up the wrong book. If, on the other hand, you'd like to know more about what happened in these three encounters and how you can keep from making these and similar mistakes yourself, get a cup of tea, find a comfortable chair, and read on.

## How Do I Know if I Need This Book? Take the Test!

If you work in a public-facing job, a job that involves regular interaction with the general public, and if a good number of the members of the public you deal with don't speak English well, then you're a good candidate for this book. The other criterion would be how aware you are of the most common mistakes people like you make when they speak English to people with limited English. To help you find out how aware you are, we've put together a little test which you will find in Appendix B. If you take that test right now, you'll know very soon whether you need to keep reading.

## I'd Like to Help But...

Like most readers, you are probably well intentioned. You are sympathetic to the challenges limited-English speakers face or you would not have picked up a book with this title and subtitle, and you would like to learn how you can help. You're just not sure you're motivated enough or have enough time to read a whole book on the subject.

That's a very legitimate concern—and the reason this book has deliberately been kept to just over 148 pages, not including the appendixes. It shouldn't take you more than three or four hours to read, and less time if you choose to read certain chapters and not others. Think of it this way: most meetings you go to last for at least an hour, sometimes 90 minutes. In the time it takes you to attend three or four meetings, you could finish this book.

## *Origins*

This book grew out of a 90-minute segment on language I used to do as part of a one-day workshop on cultural differences for county government employees in the United States, specifically in the Washington, DC area. The language segment focused on common mistakes native speakers make when talking to limited-English speakers and offered advice on how participants could improve these interactions. At the end of these workshops, I'd always ask participants to name one thing they learned that day that was especially helpful, their key takeaway (as training types call it). Much to my surprise (and chagrin), many participants completely overlooked the wonderful activities about cultural differences I had presented (my specialty) and said the segment on language helped them the most.

That hurt, naturally—I am much more of a culture guy than a language guy—but I came to understand why. It wasn't that participants didn't find the cultural activities helpful or memorable (most participants, anyway), but that the language segment was so immediate, so real for them; they instantly identified with the mistakes I was pointing out, and they were practically desperate for my suggestions. Their reactions were so striking that I realized clearly this is a big, unfilled need. And I wondered if I could fill it.

Whether or not I have, readers will know soon enough if their conversations with limited-English speakers start to improve.

# PART 1

# A FEW FUNDAMENTALS

The meat of this book, the reason you probably picked it up in the first place, is in Part 2—especially Chapters 4–9—where we offer 50 pieces of very practical advice on how to talk to speakers of limited English, as promised in the subtitle. And you are, of course, free to skip to Part 2 and start reading.

But we hope you'll take the time and read these three early chapters. While Part 2 can certainly stand on its own, all the advice you'll find there will make much more sense if you understand what's behind it, the specific challenges people with limited English face, and how the suggestions in these pages can help them. Once you understand the factors that are driving this advice, you will be much more motivated to start applying it.

Here in Part 1, then, we offer a detailed analysis of what often occurs during a typical exchange between native and limited-English speakers (Chapter 1), a profile of the mind-set and everyday reality of many immigrants (Chapter 2), and a polite debunking of the common misconceptions about speaking to people with limited English (Chapter 3). With all this as background, Part 2 will come alive for you.

Meanwhile, if you're wondering what all the mistakes were in those three scenarios in the Introduction, then turn to Appendix C.

1

# THE ENCOUNTER

*To inquire was comparatively easy... The trouble started when the Turkis answered. They all spoke at once, in loud voices, and none of them seemed capable of conceiving that the world held human beings unfamiliar with their language.*

—Peter Fleming
*News from Tartary*

If you're like most native-English speakers who work in public-facing jobs, you assume that when you interact with someone with limited English and whose language you do not speak—Spanish or Arabic, let's say—it won't be long before you reach an impasse, the moment when the conversation comes to a stop and you will need to look for an interpreter, call a translation hotline, or maybe use a phone app of one sort or another. In a lot of cases, you'll simply give up. After all, the English of the person you're speaking to can't suddenly get better, and you can't suddenly start speaking Mandarin.

Quite true as far as it goes; it just doesn't go far enough. To be sure, their English isn't going to magically get better; in fact it will probably get worse during the encounter, as we will explain later. And sure enough, you're not suddenly going to acquire the gift of tongues and start speaking Farsi or Polish.

But these two are not the only scenarios; there is a third one, something *else* that could happen in these encounters which can completely transform the exchange and greatly increase the chances of a satisfying outcome, for you and for the limited-English speaker you're trying to serve. And the good news is that the third scenario is not especially difficult and is entirely in your hands.

What most of us native speakers often overlook in these situations is that the problem here may not be only or even primarily the limited English of the other person; it could be *our English*. And while we certainly can't do anything about the former, we can do a great deal about the latter.

"*Our* English?" you're asking. "But there's nothing wrong with our English!" True enough, except for the inconvenient fact that the person you're talking to can't understand you. "That may be," you reply. "But what's that got to do with me?" Which is just the question this book was written to answer.

But we're getting ahead of ourselves. Before we look at a typical encounter, let's take a step back and first describe just who the native speakers are that we're talking about here (the primary audience for this book) and who these speakers of limited English are.

## DEFINITION OF NATIVE SPEAKERS

In these pages a native speaker refers to someone who grows up in an English-speaking country and learns English as their mother tongue.

Moreover, many of these individuals may also have not had much experience conversing with people who speak limited English, unless they have traveled extensively, have lived abroad, or have worked in a multilingual environment. Hence, they typically do not realize that limited-English speakers often have trouble understanding them, and they are largely unaware of the need to adjust their spoken English with such folks, nor have they had any practice doing so.

Finally, we should point out that in many, perhaps most, cases native English speakers are not bilingual; that is, they normally do not speak any language other than their native English. This is true, for example, of all but 18 percent of Americans and all but 39 percent of the British. This is significant because people who have never learned a second language have never had the experience of being a limited-_____ speaker (fill in the blank), trying to understand native speakers of that language and to make themselves understood to native speakers. The experience of being a limited speaker themselves would automatically attune them to some of the challenges limited-English speakers face.

"Brits and Americans aren't very good at taking part in International English," Lynne Murphy writes in her book *The Prodigal Tongue*.

> The monolingualism of the typical native English speaker is a factor. Not having much experience at communicating in a second language, Brits and Americans tend to speak to English learners just the same as they would to native speakers, or to exaggerate in some unhelpful, unnatural way.[1]

While this does not apply to every native English speaker or monolingual, if you can relate even a little, and if you work in any type of "public-facing" job, then you are the person for whom this book is written. By public-facing we mean any job in which you have face-to-face contact with members of the general public. Public-facing jobs are usually public-service jobs, the most common of which would be jobs in the government sector, whether national, state or province, county, or municipal, in virtually all departments and divisions. Another large contingent of public-facing jobs would be in the health-care sector: hospitals, emergency rooms, outpatient clinics, doctors' offices, and elder-care facilities. Many bank employees are public facing, as are many jobs in the food and hospitality industries. And most other sectors have some jobs that are public facing even if the sector is not.

## DEFINITION OF LIMITED-ENGLISH SPEAKERS

In these pages a limited-English speaker is any individual living or working in your country, whether permanently or temporarily, who grew up learning a language (their mother tongue) other than English and whose exposure to English is such that the individual speaks English poorly and understands only the simplest exchanges.* In most cases this person is foreign-born, a national of another country who grew up there and subsequently

---

* To avoid the awkward, repetitive use of he/she, him/her, and his/her, we are using the plural pronouns—they, them, and their—to refer back to singular antecedents. For example, *somebody left their phone on the table*.

immigrated or perhaps fled to your country or has come to work there on a temporary basis.

Some people who speak English as a second language are bilingual, others speak it very well, and still others speak it moderately well. None of the folks in these three categories should have much difficulty understanding native English speakers, and none of these meets our definition of a limited-English speaker. But many individuals have not lived in your country very long or may have lived there for some time but in immigrant subcultures, interacting primarily with other natives of their home country, speaking only their first language—many of these individuals speak limited English, and they often have trouble understanding native speakers.

Someone who speaks limited English can ask and understand a few simple questions, can reply briefly and understand brief replies to such questions, and can with some difficulty carry on a simple conversation for perhaps three or four sentences. After that, they begin to encounter words they do not know, expressions they are not familiar with, and other confusing language habits of native speakers, and the conversation often goes where they cannot follow. The folks we are talking about cannot understand a radio broadcast, a television show, or a movie, or read most documents written for native speakers. In many of the most common conversations, they are quickly out of their depth, become embarrassed and agitated, and resort to some form of the phrase that gives this book its title, "Sorry, no English."

They are "sorry," to be sure, but it's not quite true that they have "no English." They have limited English, and if you're not careful, your English can quickly exceed their limits. But if you do the right things, as we will see presently, it doesn't have to.

## The Numbers—The US

In the United States, the term "limited English" comes from the US Census Bureau's American Community Survey which asks respondents aged five and above who report speaking a language other than English at home to assess whether they speak English:

- not at all
- not well
- well
- very well

The Census Bureau considers anyone who self-assesses as speaking English less than very well to be "limited-English proficient," in other words, all the wells, not-wells, and not-at-alls. In this book, however, with regard to the United States, we define limited-English speakers *only as those in the not-well category.* We are not talking about those who speak very well or well, and we are likewise not talking about those who have no English at all (nothing you could do, after all, will help that group understand you).

In trying to put a number to this not-well group, our best source remains the Census Bureau, from whose data we can do a bit of extrapolating to arrive at a rough estimate of the not-wells. In 2019, the last date for which data is currently available, the number of limited-English proficient (LEP) people in the country—everyone but the very-wells—was reported as 26 million, or approximately 9 percent of the total population.[2]

Assuming some kind of a bell-curve distribution for the three LEP groups—the wells, not-wells, and not-at-alls—the groups at each extreme (wells and not-at-alls) would account at most for 50 percent of the total number of 26 million. The remaining group, the not-wells, would account for the other 50 percent, or close to 13 million folks. These not-wells are the focus of this book.

But that number does not account for the total of not-wells in the country since we can be fairly certain that most of those who responded to the Census Bureau's American Community Survey were in the United States legally. Our figure of 13 million, then, does not include anyone who is undocumented or unauthorized. In 2015 that number, according to the Pew Research Center, was 11 million, or 3.4 percent of the total US population, with Mexico accounting for just over half the total.[3] Not all these individuals would be classified as limited-English speakers, of course, but almost certainly it would be a much higher percentage than those in the legal group, probably closer to 75 percent or more than 8 million. If we add this 8 million to our earlier total of 13 million, we get a new total of 21 million not-wells, or just under 9 percent of the total US population. These are the limited-English speakers we are talking about in these pages so far as the United States is concerned.

For the record, the 11 states with the greatest number of LEP speakers are:

| California | 17% of all LEP speakers |
| Texas | 13% |
| New York | 13% |
| Florida | 12% |
| New Jersey | 12% |
| Hawaii | 12% |
| Nevada | 12% |
| Massachusetts | 9% |

| New Mexico  | 9% |
| Illinois    | 8% |
| Connecticut | 8% |

Nearly two-thirds (64 percent) of all LEPS are of Latino origin, with Spanish as the most common mother tongue.

## The Numbers—The UK, Canada, Australia

The Migration Observatory tracks the use and proficiency of the English language among foreign-born migrants in the United Kingdom. Foreign-born migrants are not the only source of limited-English speakers in the country, of course, but they are a major source, and their number has almost doubled in recent years, from 5.3 million in 2004 to 9.5 million in 2019, or 14 percent of the current population. When surveyed in the 2011 census, the last time the language question was asked, the vast majority of migrants, 89 percent, reported speaking English well or very well, with the remaining 11 percent, or nearly 1 million, speaking limited English. Since the 2011 census was conducted before some recent migrant surges, such as from Romania and Bulgaria, the percent of limited-English speakers in the UK is doubtless higher at the present time. It is noteworthy in this context that in 2018 the Observatory reported that half of all foreign-born migrants (over 4.5 million) spoke a language other than English at home. While this is not itself an indicator of low English proficiency on the part of these individuals, it suggests that many of them most likely speak their mother tongue much better than English.[4]

Estimating the number of limited-English speakers in Canada is immensely complicated by the fact that there are two official languages, French and English, spoken by 23 percent and 75 percent of the population respectively, with 18 percent of the population bilingual. While many native French speakers—almost 43 percent in Quebec in the 2011 census, for example—can also speak English, an unknown percentage of French speakers there and elsewhere in Canada doubtless have some degree of limited proficiency, meaning that native English speakers might want to follow some of the advice offered in these pages when speaking to many native French speakers.

In 2016 just under 2 percent of the Canadian population, approximately 650,000, did not speak either official language, while 20 percent of the population (in 2011) reported speaking a language other than French or English at home—two populations which likely struggle to varying degrees trying to communicate in English. For Toronto, the numbers were higher; in 2018, 5 percent of Torontonians could not speak English, and the mother tongue of 43 percent of Toronto residents was neither English nor French.[5]

In Australia in 2016, 3.5 percent of the population self-reported speaking "another language and English not well or not at all," an increase of 0.5 percent over the 2011 census. By 2018 that number was estimated to be just over 1 million. In 2016, 20.8 percent of the population reported speaking a language other than English at home, another group of people among whom there are bound to be speakers of limited English.[6]

## THE ENCOUNTER

The most common situation this book has been written to address involves an interaction in a public setting between a

native speaker of English and a speaker with limited English.
We described three such situations in our introduction, and we
reprint the first one here:

You work at the reception desk in an office that offers free
prenatal care to low-income pregnant women. Mrs. Garcia has
come in this morning to register for the office's service, and you
speak to her as follows:

| | |
|---|---|
| You: | Good morning, Mrs. Garcia. What brings you here today? |
| Mrs. Garcia: | Excuse me? |
| You: | How can I help you? |
| Mrs. Garcia: | I need your service. |
| You: | Of course. Here are some forms for you to fill out. We'll also need to verify your income. |
| Mrs. Garcia: | Yes. |
| You: | The doctor's running behind this morning, but I'll try to squeeze you in. Sorry for all the red tape, but you'll get through it. Just bring the forms back to me when you're finished. |
| Mrs. Garcia: | Yes. |
| You: | Do you have any questions? |
| Mrs. Garcia: | No. Thank you. |

As we said earlier, the native speaker made a rather large
number of "mistakes" here, in the sense of using vocabulary
and resorting to other common native-speaker habits that often
confuse someone with minimal English. We will describe those
mistakes, along with numerous others, in the chapters which follow, but here we invite the reader to try to see this exchange

from the perspective of the limited-English speaker. If you understand what's going through Mrs. Garcia's mind and what she is feeling as she stands there in front of you, you begin to understand the challenges many of the not-wells face and may wonder what you can do to help.

The first thing to realize is that Mrs. Garcia would rather be almost any place but standing in your office this morning. Think about it: She speaks limited English; almost all her previous experiences in situations like this have gone badly, meaning she was quickly out of her depth linguistically and did not understand what was being said; and she expects the same thing—to be making a fool of herself—to happen again any minute. Naturally, she feels nervous, anxious, and tense. Wouldn't you?

Which brings us to our next question: Why on earth would Mrs. Garcia, knowing all this, come to your office by herself? Surely someone in her family, a close friend, or a neighbor speaks better English and could accompany her and translate? If she has come alone, risking almost certain humiliation, then clearly she is not in any position to wait for more favorable circumstances. In short, she really needs the service you offer—and she needs it now. And the urgency of her need can only add to her agitation and anxiety.

Now let's assume there are other people in the vicinity, either sitting nearby, waiting to be called up to the window, or standing in line. So now Mrs. Garcia realizes her looming humiliation is going to take place in public. If Mrs. Garcia could, she'd leave as soon as she saw the other people waiting and try to come back later when the office wasn't so busy. If she persists under these circumstances, then this is one determined lady, willing to risk considerable embarrassment for the cause that has brought her to you. So far, so bad.

And now it begins: "Good morning, Mrs. Garcia. What brings you here today?"

What brings me here? My car? My friend? The bus? The train? Why do they need to know how I got here? Just one sentence in and she's already floundering. If I'm lucky, she might be thinking, we can pretend this isn't happening.

"Excuse me?"

And she *is* lucky because at least you don't simply repeat the question but ask it in a different form:

"How can I help you?" (Kudos to you.)

What a relief! Mrs. Garcia understands that question. Indeed, it's a phrase limited-English speakers learn very early on.

But then comes the deluge:

"Here are some forms for you to fill out. We'll also need to verify your income. The doctor's running behind this morning, but I'll try to squeeze you in. Sorry for all the red tape, but you'll get through it. Just return the forms back to me when you're finished."

You've said a total of 10 things that Mrs. Garcia has potentially not understood (see Appendix C), and now she has to decide what to do next. Normally people in these situations ask you to repeat what you've said, but in this particular instance you have said so many things it's hard for Mrs. Garcia to know where to start. Ask you to repeat what, exactly? She also knows that if she asks you to repeat, this is going to take some additional time, and the people in line behind her are going to get frustrated. Finally, she naturally assumes that you too are going to get frustrated when she doesn't understand you and requires more of your time *with all those people waiting*. If Mrs. Garcia was already anxious going into this conversation, she is even more agitated now.

What happens next is most unfortunate—and all but

inevitable. When people are agitated and nervous, their ability to speak in a second language is greatly diminished, *no matter how well they speak*. And if they are like Mrs. Garcia and don't speak very well to begin with, then whether she had enough English to converse with you as this exchange opened—this book will maintain that she did—once the situation begins to deteriorate and she becomes increasingly confused, Mrs. Garcia will not be able to access whatever English she has, limited or not.

In short, while she might in fact have enough English to talk to you under ideal circumstances, when Mrs. Garcia is feeling embarrassed, stressed, and otherwise agitated, her ability to speak English in these circumstances will be seriously compromised. With no end to her embarrassment in sight, the chief concern of Mrs. Garcia now is no longer prenatal care but how to extricate herself from this situation as soon as possible.

In his book *Living Poor* about his Peace Corps experience in Ecuador, the writer Moritz Thomsen describes an experience he had that Mrs. Garcia would certainly recognize. Thomsen was on an overcrowded bus in a rural area when a none-too-sober local got on and, there being no seats, squatted in the aisle, put his head in Thomsen's lap, and passed out. The man slept for some time and then awoke and directed "a torrent of Spanish" at Thomsen:

> My God, I couldn't understand a word he said, not one single word, and I had to sit there mile after mile, smiling like a dummy.... The other passengers were watching me with expressions of increasing pity as it dawned on them...that the gringo was a half-wit. My friend finally realized it too and gazed at...me, the escaped

but harmless crackbrain, wandering lost, dazed, and speechless in a strange and distant country.[7]

Mrs. Garcia would certainly sympathize.

As Mrs. Garcia leaves without completing her business with you, you might consider how her encounter has affected her. It has confirmed her fears about how these situations always unfold (Why do I bother?); it has undermined her self-esteem; and it has dealt yet another blow to her self-confidence.

But what if Mrs. Garcia, thanks to you, had been able to successfully complete her encounter in your office? Imagine how she might feel then. Her fears and worries about how she was ever going to be able to cope in your country would be diminished; her self-esteem would have shot up; and her self-confidence—for once—would have gotten a real boost. And she would have gotten the important service she needed.

All things being equal, wouldn't you rather be someone who is responsible for the second set of outcomes rather than the first?

*They spell it Vinci and pronounce it Vinchy. Foreigners always spell better than they pronounce.*

—Mark Twain
*The Innocents Abroad*

*If the English language made any sense, lackadaisical would have something to do with a shortage of flowers.*

—Doug Larson

2

# PROFILE OF A
# LIMITED-ENGLISH SPEAKER

*When I was suddenly thus cast on foreign land, I found myself deprived of the use of speech and hearing; and, during some weeks incapable not only of enjoying the pleasures of conversation, but even of asking or answering a question in the common intercourse of life....From a man I was again degraded to the dependence of a schoolboy...and helpless and awkward as I have ever been. My condition seemed as destitute of hope as it was devoid of pleasure.*

—Edward Gibbon
*Memoirs*

It's a truism in marketing that the better you understand your customers, the better you can sell to them. You're not exactly selling anything in your public-facing position, but the better you understand the mindset of foreign-born citizens and how they are feeling as they stand in front of you, the better you will be able to serve them. In this chapter we consider a number of factors which influence the expectations and ultimately the behavior of many limited-English speakers, factors that many native speakers would not necessarily be aware of.

## CULTURE SHOCK

Many native speakers, like yourself, perhaps, have not immigrated to and started a new life in a foreign country. Hence, you may not be able to fully grasp what recent immigrants go through as they adapt to a new country and culture and begin interacting with the locals. To be sure, not all limited-English speakers are recent immigrants, but many of them are (that's why their English is limited), and for as long as a year or more they may be going through what is commonly known as culture shock.

### The Elements of Culture Shock

Briefly stated, culture shock is the cumulative impact of having to adjust to so many things that are new and different when a person leaves their home country and moves to another country to live and work. The list of these adjustments is lengthy and usually includes but is not limited to the following:

- A new spoken and written language
- A new job—or no job
- Different customs and social norms
- A foreign education system
- New websites and online search terms
- Immigration and visa requirements

- Unfamiliar laws and regulations
- New coworkers and a new boss
- A different climate
- Different food (and the absence of home-culture food)
- Being separated from and missing friends and family
- Dealing with the loss of family members and close friends
- Having no friends yet in the new country
- Meeting and getting to know all new people
- Learning one's way around a new town or city
- The loss of many daily routines
- Learning the protocols for a myriad of new situations:
    - Food stores and all other retail stores, including online
    - Banks
    - Barbershops and hair salons
    - Restaurants
    - The post office
    - The cinema
    - Parks and other recreational venues
    - Hospitals and clinics
    - Government offices
    - Parking garages and street parking
    - Driving regulations
    - Public transportation (buses, trains)

## The Impact of Culture Shock

Every day new immigrants find themselves in circumstances and situations they have never faced before in their new country, make many mistakes, embarrass themselves, become frustrated, and want to go home. They are adults with what feels like the coping skills of small children.

The emotional and psychological consequences of culture shock include:

- Loss of self-esteem and self-respect
- Loss of self-confidence
- Feelings of inadequacy and self-doubt
- Depression
- Loneliness
- Anger and irritability
- Impatience
- Frustration: everything takes so long, and some things aren't even possible
- Humiliation at making so many mistakes
- Mental fatigue from listening to and trying to speak in English all day
- Emotional exhaustion

## Loss of Self

There is one additional dimension of culture shock, one that is related to language, that merits more than just a bullet point: what might be called loss of self or perhaps loss of personality. When you cannot speak another language very well, you literally cannot express yourself. You are unable to reveal or otherwise make known all the various facets of your personality that comprise your identity.

Let's say you have a very good sense of humor, or that you

are especially good at listening to and sympathizing with people, or that you immediately make other people feel at ease. To the extent that these qualities are made known to others through language, then any limits to your language are limits on your ability to fully express who you are. And if you can't express who you are, how can anyone really know you? This is not typical loneliness, the loneliness of not knowing anyone else, it is the loneliness of not *being known* by others.

The great British traveler and travel writer Freya Stark felt this acutely on her many journeys in the Middle East. "What I find trying in a country which you do not understand and where you cannot speak," she writes, "is that you can never be *yourself*. You are English, or Christian, or Protestant, or anything but your individual *you*....[1]

If you bear in mind that the person standing in front of you may be feeling some of these common effects of culture shock, then their behavior may make more sense to you. And for your part, as you better understand this person's mental and emotional state, you may be motivated to adjust your behavior to help them feel more comfortable. And the single greatest adjustment you can make in your circumstances is to tweak your English to bring it more in line with the level of the person you're speaking to.

The preceding discussion should also help you understand why some of the folks standing in front of you have such limited English; it is just one of numerous challenges on their plate and quite likely not even the most urgent or important one. While improving their English would probably do more than any other single thing to mitigate the effects of culture shock, it may not be a priority. People who are in the midst of culture shock and who are also working two part-time jobs to support their family, or so they can send money back home, or are looking after young children trying to adjust to a new country and a new school, or are taking care of a sick or elderly parent—people in these circumstances may not feel like attending an English class at the end of their day. And even if they did attend, what are their chances of staying awake?

## Foreign-born Refugees

For a certain class of the foreign-born, culture shock is the least of their worries. In recent years in particular, the number of people leaving their home country involuntarily, fleeing war and religious or political oppression, has risen dramatically. These people have not chosen to be immigrants, nor have they chosen to live in your country, though they are no doubt very grateful for the opportunity.

Many of them have witnessed unspeakable horrors and may have lost or been separated from members of their family. Their homes may have been destroyed or severely damaged or confiscated. Very often they have to leave in a hurry and can only take the barest minimum of possessions and may not have access to their bank accounts. They may be malnourished or have serious health problems. They may be in transit for months, in refugee camps, for example, before they arrive in your country. Their lives have been turned upside down.

It is one thing to choose to leave your country and go elsewhere in search of a better life. It is quite another to be forced to flee, in some cases to save your life. These individuals will be subject to culture shock, but the traumas of their flight, of losing or being separated from loved ones, and of losing their liveli-hood will weigh much more heavily. If they can get to the point where culture shock is their biggest concern, they will count themselves lucky.

On this note we might add that refugees who are fleeing war, religious persecution, or political oppression are often highly educated, middle-class professionals who led comfortable lives and worked in high-status positions. Now, in your country, they are taxi drivers and security guards, barely making enough to feed themselves and their families. From living near the top of the socio-economic ladder back home, they have fallen far. Their feelings of self-worth and self-esteem have taken a terrible beating. Learning English may be a very distant prospect.

## IMMIGRANT SUBCULTURES

For obvious reasons, limited-English speakers are more likely to be recent arrivals and, therefore, more likely to be in the midst of culture shock. At the same time, it must be said that some immigrants with limited English have lived in your country for some time, several years perhaps, and still speak English poorly. These folks got over their culture shock some time ago, so why hasn't their English improved?

A person's English can improve in two ways: by studying English and taking a language class or through regular exposure to and interaction with native speakers, in other words, through practice. While the former can help to a certain extent, it needs to be combined with the latter—people need to *use* what they learn in class—to be truly effective. But in some cities and counties, there is such a large and well-established immigrant subculture that immigrants can live and even work in these locations with minimal or sometimes even no contact with native speakers.

According to the Census Bureau, LEP residents made up more than one-third of the entire population aged five and older in nine counties in the United States: seven in Texas, one in Alaska, and one in Florida. Two cities, New York City and Los Angeles, had more than 3 million LEP residents, and three other cities—Miami, Chicago, and Houston—had 1 million LEPS each. Together, these five cities accounted for 37 percent of the entire US LEP population.[2]

In these communities and similar ones in other countries, it is possible for limited-English speakers to spend the vast majority of their time interacting only with people who speak their mother tongue. Hence, there may not be any urgency for them to learn English and, barring some other pressing need, no motivation to do so. In this context, one additional statistic from the Census Bureau is extremely telling: in 2015, 18 percent of LEP individuals in the United States were *native born*. These 4.7 million folks have lived in the United States *since birth* and still assess themselves as speaking limited English.

In the end, it doesn't matter why some people speak limited English; it's just a fact—for at least 13 million people (in the United States, for example), the documented ones, and most likely for another 8 million, the unauthorized ones—and when these folks come into contact with native speakers in public-facing professions, the encounters don't always end well.

## THE CONCEPT OF PUBLIC SERVICE
## AND PUBLIC SERVANTS

If you occupy a public-facing position at any level of government—local, state or provincial, or federal—chances are you subscribe to three notions about your job that many limited-English speakers do not share or even understand. These notions concern:

- how you perceive your job
- how you perceive the public
- how you are perceived by the public.

To the extent that your notions are not shared by the people you serve, to that same degree you may not understand what they are expecting from you, how they believe they should behave toward you, and how they expect you to treat them. Let's examine how your views in these three areas may differ, in some cases dramatically, from those of people from many countries.

If you're a public servant in the United States or any other English-speaking country, these notions are quite straightforward:

- My job is to serve the members of the public and meet their needs, offering support, guidance, and services consistent with my job description and the mandate of my department and according to our policies and procedures. I will keep my job and enjoy advancement to the degree I meet the needs of the people I serve.

- The members of the public are my clients and customers; they pay my salary with their taxes and have every right to expect me to be courteous and competent in meeting their needs.
- The members of the public see my job as helping them and assume that is my primary motivation in carrying out my responsibilities.

In this model, civil servants keep their jobs and earn promotion based primarily on how well they meet the members of the public's needs. To be sure, this does not mean the public always get what they want from public-sector workers, that these workers are always competent, polite, and efficient, and that dealing with the bureaucracy cannot sometimes be enormously frustrating. Nevertheless, the basic concept—that public servants serve the public—is accepted by both parties and regulates the interactions between them.

## Another Model

This is not the public-service model in countries where many immigrants come from, especially those from more authoritarian countries (including dictatorships and military-led governments), such as those in some parts of the Caribbean, Central and South America, the Middle East, and Africa. In some of these countries, public servants get their jobs in large part because they know the right people, often regardless of qualifications, and they stay in their jobs as long as they stay on good terms with and address the needs of their benefactors, and as long as the political or ethnic faction (or tribe) they belong to stays in power. When a different group comes to power, those beholden to the old faction often lose their jobs, and a new set of public servants takes over. Or you may lose your position simply because the nephew of the head of your department has graduated from college and needs a job.

And this all takes place, let us not forget, in poorer countries where there is often high unemployment and where a government job, as a result, is a gift from the gods—and in any event is often only temporary. While this arrangement does not preclude the possibility of good public service, whenever the needs of the public clash with the agenda and wishes of those in power, the outcome is not always in the public's best interests. In such societies, the greater good of the whole seldom prevails over the narrow interests of the few.

Moreover, it is not uncommon in more authoritarian governments for resources intended for the public, especially money, to be diverted into private hands, severely limiting the ability of public servants to carry out their responsibilities. We should also point out that black markets and other forms of tax evasion (e.g., paying only in cash) are common in many societies, meaning that a large percentage of the public pays little or even no taxes, further handicapping the ability of the government to deliver public services, assuming, of course, that that is its primary concern.

In such a scheme, not surprisingly, once public servants are paid with whatever limited public funds may be available, there may not be much left over to spend on the actual public. Indeed, in many cases the civil servants themselves are either not paid on a regular basis or paid so poorly that they must look elsewhere to supplement their modest income. The most common form of "elsewhere" is an understanding wherein the members of the public, in return for service, will offer a small gratuity. Only those in a position to offer such a gratuity would be inclined to seek a public servant's help in the first place or be likely to receive it.

Now let us re-examine the three notions about a public servant's job based on this model.

- How you perceive your job: Your job is to somehow hold on to your job for as long as possible (you know it's not forever) and to insure it pays enough so you can support yourself and your family while putting aside some funds against the inevitable time when you will lose your job. You do all this primarily by staying in the good graces of the people to whom you owe your job and generally not being a nuisance to them, such as by complaining that you do not have the resources to serve the public, and by otherwise playing the game as they would wish you to play it. As long as you do not rock the boat, you can stay in it.

- How you perceive the public: The public is, at best, a secondary concern of yours. Members of the public can be useful if they are in a position to add to your income, but those who cannot and still ask for your help are a nuisance. In fact, they are worse than a nuisance; they are a painful, perhaps even embarrassing, reminder of how impossible it is to do your job with the limited resources at your disposal. It should not be surprising, in this reality, that whenever members of the public do ask for help, your first response will always be "no," not because that is necessarily the case but because in your circumstances "no" is the safest response, the one that will complicate your life the least since it is almost guaranteed not to get you into trouble with your superiors. It is true, incidentally, that you might at one time in your career have been somewhat sympathetic toward members of the public, but once you become a servant of the system, the less you have to do with the public the easier it will be for you. You will no longer be caught in the middle between the people who desperately need your help on the one hand and the people who get in the way of your offering it on the other. You will sleep much better.

- How you are perceived by the public: The members of the public are well aware of how the game is played, of how lucky you are to have your job, and of what you need to do to keep it. And they realize that that does not involve serving them, unless they can afford it. For the most part, then, those who cannot afford it stay away and do without. On those rare occasions when circumstances force them to approach a public servant, they know the only chance they have of getting a hearing from you is to bow and scrape, to treat you with the utmost deference and subservience, and above all to be extremely careful not to do or say anything that might annoy or frustrate you. Indeed, their mere presence in your office, people asking for what you cannot give or are afraid to give, is already frustrating enough.

To be sure, there are tens of thousands of dedicated and selfless public servants in authoritarian regimes all around the world, heroes and heroines under the circumstances, and we may perhaps have exaggerated the above description slightly to get your attention. Nor, to be fair, is political patronage unknown in most English-speaking countries, although it is almost always confined to senior government positions. At the same time, it is an undisputed fact that many of the foreign-born who come to the United States and other English-speaking countries, legally and illegally, do so, at least in part, to escape the very conditions described above.

## The Encounter Reconceived

Armed with this awareness, let's return to the encounter in your office between you and a foreign-born national and consider the implications. The first thing to remember is that this individual does not approach you feeling that they are entitled to or have a right to the help your office is there to provide. They come in, rather, as a supplicant on the off chance you may be in a good mood and take pity on them. Hence, their manner is going to be extremely respectful, deferential, even obsequious. This may make you uncomfortable, and you may even think they're being insincere and trying to suck up to you. They *are* trying, actually, but it's not insincerity; they sincerely believe this is the only way to reach you. You should not be put off by or misinterpret this behavior.

Another factor to consider here is that this individual has thought long and hard before deciding to show up in your office today, assuming nothing will come of it (other than embarrassment) unless they have some kind of leverage. If they have none and have come anyway, then they really need your help, have nowhere else to turn, and are probably very nervous. As we noted in Chapter 1, when limited-English speakers are nervous, their English becomes even more limited. This may very well complicate the encounter initially, but it's also true that when you do not appear annoyed at being approached (what they may be expecting) or at all reluctant to offer help, it may come as a tremendous relief. If this relief comes early in the encounter, it will help to relax the individual and thus help the exchange go more smoothly.

Another point to remember is the great fear this individual may have of causing any annoyance. If they think you see them as a nuisance *just for showing up and asking for something*, then in the event their conversation with you gets off to a bad start— they don't understand you or you have trouble understanding them—they will quickly become afraid, flustered, and increasingly inarticulate.

You should also remember that this individual has very low expectations of actually being helped. While their needs may be acute or they wouldn't be standing there, their experience has taught them that they shouldn't press their luck and ask for very much and be happy with whatever they get. They may in fact select a secondary matter to bring up with you and never mention a more critical need that they just assume will be too much trouble for you. If you suspect this is what is happening, you would be doing them a great kindness if, after addressing their secondary issue, you asked whether there is anything else you can do for them before they leave.

In this same context, you should also remember, for reasons explained above, that this individual is assuming your first response to their request is going to be "no," because it is always "no" in the country they come from. Back home, therefore, people like them never take "no" for a real response and ask again. And even when they get a second "no," they know from experience that persistence can sometimes pay off, that the civil servant may eventually decide at some point that saying "yes" is going to be easier than to keep arguing with this member of the public.

What this means for you is that if you are not in fact able to meet the individual's request, if the answer, in other words, *really is* "no," then your foreign-born customer may assume this is the "no" they are used to getting back home and keep making the same request over and over, or even ask to talk to your supervisor. If getting a "yes" is only a matter of persisting, then they would be foolish to take "no" for an answer. Keep this in mind when some folks with limited English continue to ask for something after you've told them no.

Not everyone who has lived under an authoritarian regime is going to be under these assumptions, but many will be and thus will have a completely different—and completely inaccurate—understanding of how people in your position see your job and what you think of the public. If you are aware of their perspective, that will help you understand some behaviors that may otherwise make no sense and in general enable you to serve your clients more effectively.

We might add that some of you may not recognize the individual we have described just above, the immigrant who is expecting little or nothing from public servants and who, therefore, is deeply appreciative and greatly relieved when you are kind, helpful, and sympathetic toward them. "What about all those people who are demanding and even rude," you may be thinking, "who expect us to do everything for them, who get upset and don't believe us when we say we can't meet that particular need or that we don't offer that particular service?"

To be sure, members of the public come in all varieties, the native-speaking and the limited-English-speaking public alike. Our aim here was to describe a kind of customer or client with whom you may not be that familiar, whose mindset and background you may not understand, and whose behavior you might sometimes misinterpret. Truly demanding and rude people are much the same the world over, and you should deal with them similarly no matter where they come from. Our only caution here would be to point out that behavior that appears rude and demanding to you—because it is rude in your culture—may not have the same meaning in another culture. In those cases the speakers have no idea they are being rude and usually have no such intention.

## The Economically Disadvantaged

We should add a note here concerning immigrants to the United States from Mexico and parts of Central America, a group that accounts for more than one-third of all limited-English speakers in the country (not including illegal immigrants). In many cases these individuals come from the poorest sectors of their society, with limited education, limited income, and limited opportunities. Indeed, these are among the reasons they want to emigrate in the first place.

In many instances, these individuals exist outside the system in their home country and may not be served at all by it or even be aware of what services may be available. They may be victims of racial or ethnic discrimination, for example, or live in remote locations not reached by government agencies. Or, if they have had encounters with public-sector employees, they may have been treated badly and as a result have long since stopped trying to avail themselves of public services.

Whatever their reasons, many of these individuals have had minimal or no experience back home dealing with government officials; they have never spent time in an office like yours or had the kind of encounter we have been talking about in these pages. They don't know how the system works in your country (or theirs, for that matter) or even what it is comprised of, don't understand what your role is, don't know how these interactions normally unfold, and don't know how they're supposed to behave. Having minimal English and not understanding what you're saying is the least of their challenges.

Accordingly, they may act very confused and be at a loss in your office, and otherwise be substantially more bewildered and disoriented than immigrants who have accessed government services back home. They may also be very passive, expecting you to approach them to ask what they need instead of approaching you to initiate the conversation.

## THE FIRST TIME

At the risk of pointing out the obvious, we might briefly mention another dimension of the encounter that is very different for the two parties. You have been doing your job for some time, and for you this encounter is completely routine and utterly unexceptional. Nothing could be more straightforward.

But for the person standing in front of you, this is likely to be the first time they have been in your office. They have no idea what to expect and no sense of the protocols involved. (See Chapter 9 on standing in line and keeping appointments.) As a result, this is a stressful, tension-filled encounter, fraught with the possibility of embarrassment, of annoying others, and of frustrating and annoying you with their lack of English and general cluelessness as to how to behave. They are nervous, agitated, and uncomfortable. If there was any way they could have avoided this interaction today, they certainly would have.

In short, they are not having anything like the experience you are having, and if you are at all inclined to project onto them what you are feeling, you would be quite mistaken.

## ONE AMONG MANY

Finally, you should keep in mind that there's a very good chance the encounter between you and the limited-English speaker in front of you is just one of several such encounters the individual has experienced today, each one chipping away at their self-confidence, compounding their feelings of inadequacy, and eroding their patience. While they might have been in good shape for the first such encounter of the day, maybe even getting through it with their limited English, each successive encounter wears them down until they reach the point where they are mentally and emotionally drained, incapable of getting through another encounter even in their first language, much less their second.

*And I can't learn the language. Nobody's ever thought of giving it an alphabet, and I'm essentially a visual type. In Africa they put me in a native hut for six months, made me live with a family, just to learn the language. It was no damned good.*

*After six months all I could do was point at things— that's what my hosts did—and when I got back to Nairobi I found I was making unequivocal gestures at the women in the Club, and that didn't go down at all well.*

—Anthony Burgess
*The Enemy in the Blanket*


*We traveled in a big truck through the nation of France on our way to Belgium, and every time we passed through a little town, we'd see these signs—"Boulangerie," "Patisserie," and "Rue" this and "Rue" that and rue the day you came here young man. When we got to our hundred and eightieth French village, I screamed at the top of my lungs: "The joke is over! English, please!" I couldn't believe a whole country couldn't speak English. One third of a nation, all right, but not a whole country.*

—Mel Brooks
Quoted in Kenneth Tynan's
*Show People*

3

# SOME COMMON
# MISCONCEPTIONS

*My head, still giddy from the motion of the ship, is con-
fused by the multiplicity of novel objects: the dress of
the people, the projecting roofs and balconies of the
houses, the filth of the streets, so strange and so dis-
gusting to an Englishman. But what is most strange is
to hear a language which conveys to me only the melan-
choly reflection that I am in a land of strangers.*

—Robert Southey
*Letters*

**M**any readers will not have *any* conceptions about
limited-English speakers, accurate or otherwise, because they
haven't thought that much about them. Fair enough. But in point
of fact, you probably do have some conceptions about people
with limited English, assuming you've ever had any dealings
with them. Or if you don't have any conceptions, then you almost
certainly have a few impressions. And these impressions, largely
subconscious, are bound to influence how you think about and

how you behave during your interactions with limited-English speakers. But if these impressions or conceptions of yours are mistaken, then they are bound to undermine your interactions with people from other cultures. One last thing we need to do to tee up Part 2, the practical-advice section of this book, is to clear up the most common misconceptions so they don't adversely affect how you do your job.


## HOW THEY'LL BEHAVE DURING THE ENCOUNTER

The first set of misconceptions deals with how you think foreign-born, limited-English speakers will behave if they don't understand you.


### They'll Tell Me If They Haven't Understood Me

This is probably the most common mistake native speakers make, and while some of the public's members may be vocal about their confusion, many others, for reasons we have discussed, will not want to express their confusion and otherwise risk causing a scene. Those who are worried about holding up the line and frustrating other customers, for example, those who are worried about frustrating you, and those who are just worried about embarrassing themselves—many of these individuals will choose to terminate the encounter rather than prolong their agony and prolong yours as well by informing you they don't understand. They might briefly try to persist, but if a second attempt goes wrong, they will become increasingly nervous and increasingly inarticulate.

## They'll Tell Me If They Don't Know What a Word Means

This is a variation on the topic above and unlikely to happen for the same reasons. Some speakers, however, may initially do this, but if they have to keep asking you about words you're using, increasing the chances of annoying you, they will back off.

## They'll Ask Me to Repeat

This is a close relative of the two preceding misconceptions and is a nonstarter for the same reasons: Asking you to repeat slows things down, takes more of your time, and probably annoys you. They might do it once, maybe even twice, but as this encounter drags on, you're probably going to display some kind of frustration. And that will be that.

## They Don't Have to Say Anything; I'll See It in Their Body Language

This is entirely possible, as even those folks who won't feel comfortable putting their confusion into words may reveal it in their facial expressions, head gestures, or other types of nonverbal communication. At the same time, these individuals are often keenly aware of the danger of betraying their emotions in just this fashion and often smile and nod their head no matter what you say to them. It would be a mistake to interpret these nonverbal cues for what they usually mean: that the person understands, is encouraged, and everything is going fine. Everything is *not* going fine, but the last thing folks want is for you to know that.

Indeed, in many cultures, especially Asian countries, people smile when they are embarrassed. I was once conducting a workshop for the sheriff's office of a suburban Washington, DC county and explained why the Asian smile can sometimes be misinterpreted. One of the participants told the story of how he had pulled over an elderly Vietnamese lady for speeding in a school zone, intending to give her a warning. As he was explaining that she should slow down when passing the school, she was smiling because she was so embarrassed. He thought this meant she was not taking his warning seriously and gave her a ticket. Maybe she *was* being disrespectful, but it's highly unlikely in those circumstances.

### I'll Know If They Have Understood Me
### Because I'll Ask Them

This sounds like a straightforward, foolproof workaround for all the previous items. If you want to find out if people have understood you and can't rely on them to let you know, just ask them. Only why would the same people who are afraid to ask you to repeat, afraid to reveal anything with their body language, and generally quite nervous about prolonging an embarrassing scene—why would these people then turn around and admit they didn't understand you?

"Fine," you may be thinking. "Then how *do* I find out if they've understood me?" Part 2 will take up just this matter in some detail. For now it's enough to realize that many of the usual ways of finding out if people are following what you're saying are not going to be as effective or even work at all with many limited-English speakers.

### They Realize I May Have Trouble Understanding Them

We haven't talked much yet in these pages about the *other* problem in the native/limited-English speaker encounter: the fact that it may also be difficult for *you* to understand *them*. While this can sometimes be a challenge and will be addressed later (see Chapter 8), the fact is that when the exchange starts to go wrong because the person cannot understand you, things often do not progress to the stage where the limited-English speaker gets to say very much. But if they do manage to carry on the conversation, they are likely to be surprised, hence flustered, when you don't understand them. This is your language after all, and even if they speak it badly, which they are normally aware of, they assume you will at least know the words, regardless of how ineptly they string them together or how strangely they pronounce them.

And you probably would know the words if you could only understand their pronunciation. But the biggest problem you will normally have understanding limited-English speakers is not their grammar but their accent. And this is not something the limited English speaker will be expecting. By and large people with limited-English have not had enough experience to realize they speak with an accent, and it will accordingly come as a most unwelcome surprise. (See Chapter 8 for more about accents.)

## SOME OTHER MISCONCEPTIONS

### *Many People Study English Back Home, So They'll Be Fine When They Get Here*

There's truth in the first half of that statement: many people do indeed study English as a second or foreign language back in their home country, often for many years. And many of these folks do indeed manage quite well when they emigrate, but many others, much to their surprise and disappointment, struggle mightily. Let's consider why.

To begin with, English language instruction in non-English-speaking countries almost always focuses on reading and writing and places much less emphasis on speaking. This is usually because in most settings the teachers themselves are not native speakers and have not had many chances to practice their spoken English. People who "learn" English from such teachers don't hear much spoken English, nor do they have any chance to speak it themselves, unless they have opportunities outside the classroom. When these folks emigrate to an English-speaking country, that may very well be the first time they have been exposed in any significant way to spoken English and the first time they themselves have had to speak English. While their ability to read and write English will certainly be a great advantage over time, in the short run many of these folks may struggle almost as much as an immigrant who has never studied English. Moreover, because of their raised expectations—they naturally assume their years of study prepared them to speak English—they may struggle more than those with no English for being caught completely off guard.

There is a second, related reason why folks who learn to read and write English abroad almost always struggle when they have to talk with native speakers: the fact that English is not especially phonetic. Many English words are not pronounced the way they are spelled: the word written *r-o-u-g-h* is pronounced *ruff*; the word written *w-o-m-e-n* is pronounced *wimen* (the *i* is pronounced as in *fish*); the letters *t-i* are usually pronounced *s-h* as in *nation* (which is *not* pronounced *nay-tee-on*). The same person who can read and understand words like *women* or *rough* may very well not recognize those two words when they hear them spoken. And they may likewise mispronounce them when they speak, thus confusing native speakers.

"Every English sound can be spelled in more than one way," Lynne Murphy has observed,

> and no alphabet letter consistently has the same pronunciation. Take one of the simplest cases: *b*. The sound /b/ can be written *b* as in *trouble*, *bb* as in *stubble*, or *bh* as in *Bhutan* or *bhangra* (an Asian-British musical style). So, we have at least three spellings of /b/. Conversely, the letter *b* sometimes symbolizes the sound /b/ and sometimes it's silent, as . . . in *debt* and in *plumber*. When we look for rules in the system, we find exceptions: don't pronounce the *b* in *plumber* but do pronounce it in *slumber*. By one count there are over a thousand ways of spelling the forty basic sounds . . . of English.[1]

On this note I might relate a personal story. The phonetic disconnect in English is the reason behind the concept of spelling bees in English-speaking countries. Words are only difficult to spell if their pronunciation isn't closely related to how they are written. Hence, a spelling bee contestant might not know that the word pronounced *miniachoor* is spelled *m-i-n-i-a-t-u-r-e* (to use an insultingly simple example).

But spelling bees make no sense (and do not exist) in countries where the language is highly phonetic, such as Italy; most Italian words sound exactly like they are written. I have a good Italian friend who is fluent in English (she once worked as an English-to-Italian translator). She loves American movies which she often rents and watches with her two Italian daughters, and she especially likes movies about English spelling competitions. For years her daughters could never see the point of these contests, since the movies were subtitled, so that when the English-speaking spelling bee moderator announced the word *miniature*, the Italian *miniatura* appeared in the subtitle at the bottom of the screen. What's so hard about that?

Before we leave this topic, we should add that while many immigrants do study English at home, millions of others do not. Remember that figure of 13 million "not wells" in Chapter 2 and the additional figure of 8 million undocumented limited-English speakers. Very few of these folks are likely to have studied English in their country of origin, certainly not those from the lower socio-economic strata of society, nor millions of refugees forced to flee their home countries.

### They Live Here Now; They'll Pick Up English Soon Enough

Many of them will, to be sure. But for reasons we have already pointed out, it may take longer than you think and may not happen at all for some folks, those who live in communities with large numbers of immigrants from their home culture. Remember, too, that other group of nearly 5 million folks who were born and grew up in the United States and who, according to the Census Bureau, nevertheless assess themselves as speaking limited English. Merely living in an English-speaking country does not guarantee speaking English well.

## They Can Take a Class

They can indeed, and many of them do. But for many others, for reasons we have touched upon, it's not that easy. They may be working two jobs or otherwise so busy during the day that the idea of attending a night class is just too daunting. Or they may want to take a class but do not have their own transportation or any other way to get to the class site. And many of these folks, especially poor and disadvantaged immigrants, may not have been in a classroom for decades and may be intimidated at the prospect. In a few cases, they may not even be literate in their first language and thus be poor candidates to learn a second one.

## Spanish Isn't that Different from English; They Shouldn't Have that Much Trouble Understanding Me

In the United States a large majority of limited-English speakers—64 percent or almost two-thirds—speak the same first language, Spanish. And Spanish and English are linguistically related; approximately 35 percent of words in English have a related word in Spanish. This is a benefit to native Spanish speakers and likewise a fact that native English speakers should be aware of and exploit, using cognates (words that exist in both languages but are spelled and pronounced somewhat differently) whenever they converse with the Spanish-speaking public. (See Appendix H for a list of the 50 most common English-Spanish cognates.)

But there are also important differences. "The phonological [sound, pronunciation] system of Spanish," one linguist has noted,

> is significantly different from that of English, particularly in the aspects of vowel sounds and sentence stress. These differences are very serious obstacles to Spanish learners...It is not surprising, therefore, that Spanish learners may have great difficulty in producing *or even perceiving* the various English vowel sounds.... Spanish [also] has a strong correspondence between the sound of a word and its spelling. The irregularity of English in this respect causes predictable problems" [italics added].[2]

English is more closely related to German in most respects and has its origins in the Germanic branch of the Indo-European language family. Close to 30 percent of all English words are derived from German, including 80 of the 100 most common.

All other things being equal, native Spanish speakers (as well as speakers of the other Romance languages—see #19 in Chapter 5) certainly have it easier than Arabic, Mandarin, or Hindi speakers, for example, when it comes to understanding English. But that does not mean that it will not take many months, or even longer, for them to pick up English when they move to your country. If you encounter them when they are still learning, their Spanish is only going to get them so far.

## If They Really Wanted To, They Could Learn English

It would be a mistake to conclude that someone with limited English is just not interested in getting any better at it. While that may be true for a minority of limited-English speakers, especially those who live in an immigrant subculture, very few foreign-born immigrants fail to see the value, hence the need, of speaking English better. If these folks continue to struggle in English, then it's almost certainly not because they're lazy or unintelligent or just don't care. There are bound to be mitigating circumstances that push improving English down their list of priorities. Rest assured that they are much more frustrated by their inability to speak English than you could ever be.

## Why Is This My Problem?

A fair question. And of course it's not your problem, at least not in the sense that it's your fault these folks don't speak English, that they can't understand you, and that you're not able to be of much help to them. And it's certainly not your responsibility to somehow fix all that. Nor is anyone expecting you to. Moreover, you may very well feel that if you went to their country, the burden would be on you to learn their language. So why should it be any different for them when they come here?

It's not. They know the burden is on them; they know how much easier their life would be if they spoke better English;

they're trying, most of them, as hard as they can; and they're not expecting or asking for your help.

But if you've read this far in these pages, then you're probably the kind of person who, all the above notwithstanding, can still accept that while this may not be your problem, you do contribute to it, and you can, accordingly, be part of the solution if you so desire.

If that describes you, then Part 2 is just what you've been waiting for.

*A different language is a different vision of life.*
                                              —Federico Fellini

*One language sets you in a corridor for life. Two languages open every door along the way.*
                                              —Frank Smith

# PART 2

# THE ADVICE

Readers will recall that the central premise of this little book is that while you can't make limited-English speakers suddenly start speaking better and you can't suddenly start speaking their mother tongue, there's a great deal you can do about *your* English. And if you do the right things, you may just make it possible for a limited-English speaker to have a successful conversation with you. Those right things comprise Part 2 of this book and take up the next five chapters. Three additional chapters in Part 2 explore other important subjects.

# 4

# JOB ONE—STAYING CALM

*I remember a song we used to sing, "Columbia, Gem of the Ocean." But I thought it was, "Columbus, Jump in the Ocean."*

—Lisa See
*On Gold Mountain*

**W**e've noted several times that while some limited-English speakers do not know enough English to have a successful encounter with you—no matter what you do or how careful you are when you speak to them—many others do know enough English. But they become nervous, for reasons we've described, and lose their ability to access even the limited English they know. Accordingly, your first and most important task as a native speaker is to do whatever you can to enable folks to stay calm and thus stand an even chance to recall and deploy their English.

An important point to keep in mind here is that the person with limited English does not enter this encounter at what we might call "0," feeling neither nervous nor not nervous. If there were a nervousness scale, from -5 (very nervous) to +5 (completely relaxed), the limited-English speaker starts out somewhere around -3 or -4. Don't think of your goal, in other words, as getting the individual to +5 but getting them to 0. To put it another way, you're not going to get the person to relax and enjoy the conversation, but you might very well help them become less nervous. If that seems like small potatoes to you (just the kind of expression, by the way, that you should never use with limited-English speakers), it certainly won't seem that way to the person you're talking to.

## 1. Smile.

Throughout the encounter your body language is going to be closely scrutinized by your limited-English interlocutor, and whatever messages your body is sending are going to be instantly decoded. Remember that this individual knows that this encounter is going to be fraught, and as a result they will be extremely sensitive to any indications that it's not going well. In this regard, your body language can speak volumes.

It's important to realize in this context that body language is not like spoken language. Before you say something, you must first think it; thus you become aware of what you're going to say in the instant before you say it. In that moment, you can choose not to say it and to say something else. In short, to a certain extent you have control over the things you say, and if you exercise that control, you can adjust your speech to the level of the limited-English speaker. Indeed, that's the central principle behind this book.

But body language is not like that; it tends to be automatic and spontaneous. It comes from inside, as it were, and is not something you think before you express. In other words, you don't have any control over it. Be that as it may, if you can at least go into your encounters wearing a smile, before there is anything for your body to respond to, that gets things off to a good start.

But as soon as the conversation begins, as soon as there is any stimulus for you to react to, your body is going to start speaking. And since you won't be aware of what it's saying, it may say things you wish it wouldn't. In this regard, the best thing you can do is to closely observe the other person's body language; if your body is sending upsetting messages, you may see that in the other person's facial expressions or other behaviors. That will be your cue to start smiling again. If you're the kind of person that can paste a smile onto your face and keep it there no matter what's happening around you, all the better.

## 2. Nod.

Another helpful piece of body language is the nod, a close cousin of smiling. Nodding is an almost universal positive gesture, a general indication that things are going well and that you are following what the other person is saying. This is very encouraging to the limited-English speaker, whether it's true or not—and especially if it is not.

## 3. Don't frown.

Frowning is obviously a nonstarter. It will be a clear indication that something's not right, just the kind of signal speakers of limited English are especially attuned to—and likewise their worst nightmare.

*4. Don't misinterpret their smile and their nod.*

We might point out that while smiling and nodding are generally interpreted everywhere as positive signs, be careful about reading too much into these two behaviors on the part of limited-English speakers. Not wanting to cause you any trouble, their instinct is to smile and nod so you'll think everything is fine, but don't be misled. It's also true as we pointed out in Chapter 3 that in some cultures people smile when they are embarrassed.


*5. Don't misinterpret the meaning of "yes."*

And while we're talking about misinterpreting positive signs, be very wary of the word *yes*. In most English-speaking countries, native speakers use the word *yes* to communicate a positive response; that someone agrees with, accepts, approves of, or understands what's being proposed or explained. *Yes* is taken to be a *reply*, in short, and accordingly, having gotten a reply, people move on to their next topic or issue.

But many limited-English speakers use *yes* to mean something much vaguer and inconclusive; it's not their reply or answer to what you're saying but merely a polite indication that they are listening to what you're saying, following along (whether they are or not), and generally appreciative of your sweet words. It is effectively the equivalent of the English expression "Uh-huh." And you should treat it exactly the way you treat *Uh-huh*: that it's not an answer but merely the sound people make to signal they're listening. In other words, just as you don't mistake a native speaker's *Uh-huh* for a reply and instead listen to what the person says when it's their turn to speak, neither should you take a limited-English speaker's *yes* for a reply and listen instead to the person's actual reply which will come *after* yes.

But that's just the problem: we native speakers hear *yes*, think it *is* the reply (because it usually is when we say it), and we move on to our next point. We neither pay any attention to what the limited-English speaker says after *yes*—their real response—nor in most cases even give the person the chance to say anything after *yes* because while we would naturally pause after *Uh-huh* to let the other person speak, we don't pause after *yes* because the person *has* spoken.

The advice, then, is not to pay much attention to *yes* and to be sure to pause and give the person a chance to say something else before moving on to your next item for discussion. The same advice, by the way, applies to common synonyms for *yes*, such as *sure* and *okay*.

You should also keep in mind that whether *yes* really means *yes*, limited-English speakers know they will never disappoint anyone or cause any frustration by saying *yes*—to whatever someone says. After all, everyone likes to hear *yes*; it means things are moving along, I'm making myself clear, we're on the same page, and we're all getting along famously.

In short, never take *yes* for an answer: always probe to see if the person really is following what you're saying or just trying to be agreeable.

### 6. Get the person out of a line.

If the service you provide involves people standing in a line in front of you, try to find a way to get the limited-English speaker out of the line so you can talk to them alone. Why? When there are people standing behind your customer, that person becomes nervous even before the encounter starts. They know that if there are problems, if they don't understand you or you have difficulty understanding them, that's going to slow things down, and the people waiting are not going to be happy. If you can somehow remove that stress from the encounter, it will go a long way toward reducing your customer's agitation.

Moreover, the person may very well sense why you are doing this, to save them discomfort and embarrassment, and realize how kind you are. When your customer realizes they're dealing with a kind, sympathetic person, with someone who understands what they're feeling, that will make them relax even more.

## 7. Create some privacy.

In line with #6 above, you should take advantage of any means you may have of moving the encounter out of a place where people waiting in line or just sitting in the waiting area can over-hear it. Now it becomes a private exchange just between you and the other person. It might still be an embarrassing encounter in some respects for the person with limited English, but at least now it's a private embarrassment rather than a public one. Given this advice, you might want to anticipate this scenario and iden-tify a place in your work area that can be used for taking some-one aside whenever the need arises.

## 8. Reschedule the encounter.

This will depend a lot on the circumstances, but in some cases, especially when it is very busy in your office, you might want to offer the limited-English speaker the choice of coming back later when it's not so busy, hence not so stressful. Naturally, if the person is in a hurry or otherwise extremely eager to get your help, this might just make things worse. On the other hand, it could be an immense relief to know that when they come back, you will not be under such pressure, and your customer will accordingly feel more relaxed.

If you decide to make this offer, you should carefully explain why, that it's very busy now and "you might be more comfortable coming back (name the time) when you and I can take as much time as you need." If you don't explain why you're doing this, the person might very well feel you're just trying to get rid of them.

### 9. Assure the person that you've got plenty of time.

If the individual is worried that they're taking too much of your time, they will be reassured if you indicate that you're not in a hurry. Obviously, this won't be so convincing if there is a line of people waiting, but if it's just you and your customer (maybe even somewhere private), then knowing they can take as much of your time as they need will be immensely calming.

You should consider saying this, by the way, even if it's not true—even if you do not in fact have all that much time—for three reasons: first, it telegraphs your sympathy and kindness; second, it enables the person to relax and perhaps understand you better; and third, if the person is relaxed and understands you, this encounter is in fact going to be over sooner and not take so much of the time you do not have.

## 10. Take the blame.

If the person is clearly having trouble understanding you, they're naturally going to assume it's their fault and become agitated. And while it may be their fault (for the most part, anyway), if you take responsibility for the trouble that's occurring, that's going to make the person feel much better. You can say things like: "I know I'm not being very clear." "I'm sorry to cause you trouble." "Please excuse me for taking so much of your time." Granted, the person is going to know this really isn't true, but they're going to be so grateful to you for shouldering the blame that they're bound to feel more relaxed.

I once heard a native speaker say to a client: "You're doing just fine. At least you know my language, but I don't speak a word of yours. So you're not the problem here." I'm willing to bet that particular limited-English speaker never forgot that.

## 11. Praise their English.

There's not much you could say to limited-English speakers that would be more comforting and reassuring than to compliment their English. They're standing there, after all, knowing how poorly they speak and how much trouble they're going to cause, and suddenly you tell them how well they're doing! Once again, they know this can't really be true, but it's such a nice thing for you to say that they're immediately going to feel better about this situation. They know they're in the hands of a very considerate person.

*12. Write down any words people are having trouble understanding.*

Because English is not phonetic, because many words are not pronounced the way they are spelled (see Chapter 3), people who don't recognize a word when they hear it may know it when they see it. *Receipt* may sound like *reseat*; *stomach* may sound like *stuhmuck*; *caution* may sound like *cawshun*. When you write down difficult words and the person recognizes them, you can not only continue the conversation, you've also given the limited-English speaker reason to hope that this conversation does not have to be so difficult for either of you.

*13. Watch their body language.*

Earlier we urged you to be careful of your body language, lest you inadvertently send signals you would prefer not to send, such as those which betray that you're frustrated or becoming impatient. You should also be alert to body language from the limited-English speaker indicating that they're becoming nervous or not following the conversation. For example, you can usually see confusion (a frown) or complete lack of comprehension (a blank look) in a person's facial expressions. If the person is fidgeting, passing their weight back and forth from one leg to another, that can signal nervousness. If you can detect nervousness, then you can try to apply the other advice in this chapter to help the person relax. But you have to be on the lookout.

### 14. Help them find the word or phrase they're looking for.

In many cases you know what the person is struggling to say but somehow can't quite manage. If you step in and supply the word they're trying to remember, that can speed things along and help reduce their anxiety in the process. Some observers have suggested that if you keep finishing people's sentences for them, they'll get the point—this conversation is taking too long—and *that* will make them nervous. This is possible, but in my experience, any help you can give is usually appreciated. Once again, the mere fact that you're trying to help sends a very soothing signal.

### 15. Ask for help from someone who is better at this.

As a last resort, you might want to ask for help from someone in your office who has more experience talking to limited-English speakers. This might be someone who has had more exposure to the person's first language, someone who has learned or speaks a second language (but not the person's mother tongue because in that case they can translate and your encounter would not be happening in the first place), or just someone who has lived overseas and had practice speaking English in a country where it is not the first language. It would be a good idea if your office could identify such people ahead of time, so you know where to turn when you run out of ideas.

*Mother had, after considerable mental effort, managed to commit to memory two or three Greek words. This lack of vocabulary had a restrictive effect on her conversations at the best of times, but when she was faced with the ordeal of exchanging small talk with a murderer, she promptly forgot all the Greek she knew.*

—Gerald Durrell
*The Corfu Trilogy*

# 5

# WORD CHOICE—WATCH YOUR LANGUAGE

*Avoid unfamiliar words as a sailor avoids the rocks.*
—Julius Caesar
*The Gallic Wars*

If you've managed to help the limited-English speaker in front of you feel a bit more relaxed, you've already accomplished a great deal. You've created the best possible environment for them to listen to you and to access and apply whatever English they know.

But now the time has come for you to start talking, and this is the point where things can easily go wrong. There are, as we'll see in the next three chapters, many ways you can complicate the encounter, but one of the most critical is the simple matter of your vocabulary, of the words you use when you speak.

### 16. Don't use phrasal verbs.

This is arguably the single most important piece of advice in this book. If vocabulary is one of the biggest problems for limited-English speakers, then phrasal verbs are one of the biggest problems posed by vocabulary.

If you're like most readers, you have no idea what phrasal verbs are, much less that you use them all the time. A phrasal verb consists of a verb plus a preposition, or sometimes an adverb. Most consist of two words, but some are three. Here are a few common phrasal verbs:

| | | |
|---|---|---|
| do over | call on | keep from |
| count on | bring up | drop by |
| call off | see through | cut off |
| give up | give in | look down on |
| look out | find out | see to |

You can probably sense the problem here: the words don't mean what they say. That is, when the preposition is added to the verb, the resulting phrase bears little or no relation to what the verb means by itself, or the preposition for that matter. Take *count on*, for example. *Count* is easy: 1, 2, 3. And everyone knows *on*. But *count on* has nothing to do with counting; it means, rather, to rely or depend on. If you say "Don't count on it" to someone, you're not saying they should do their counting on something else; you're telling them not to expect something to happen.

To put all this another way, in phrasal verbs the parts bear no relation to the whole. So even if you know the parts, what *count* means and what *on* means, you will still have no idea what *count on* means. You either know the expression, because you have learned it, or you don't, but you won't understand it simply because you know the meaning of the individual components.

Most languages have their equivalent of phrasal verbs, combinations of words which, to put it simply, just don't add up. They are, as a consequence, among the hardest things to understand in a foreign language and usually one of the last things one learns. One learns them over time, hearing them repeatedly and eventually figuring them out. (*Figure out* is another phrasal verb.)

Phrasal verbs pose one of the two or three most significant challenges to limited-English speakers. Appendix D lists 60 of the most common phrasal verbs in English, but there are thousands. There are so many that it's difficult to say three or four sentences in a row without using at least one.

Phrasal verbs would not be a problem or otherwise merit all this attention if you could count on (!) limited-English speakers to ask you what you mean when you use one. Some folks may, of course, and others might ask the meaning of a couple of phrasal verbs, but they're not going to be a nuisance and ask every time. Thus, the burden of solving the phrasal-verb problem ultimately falls on you (or doesn't get solved, as the case may be).

The only foolproof solution is to catch yourself in the act of using a phrasal verb, stop, and then rephrase. This is much easier said than done, of course, because who of us listens to ourselves that closely? If you're lucky you may get a cue from the limited-English speaker who suddenly gets a blank look on their face. But otherwise, you're on your own.

Rephrasing is easy, by the way. If you'd like to try it, here are a few phrasal verbs from the list on the previous page. Write your revision on the line provided, and then check the suggestions for these and other phrasal verbs in the list in Appendix D.

1. do over _____
2. call on _____
3. call off _____
4. give up _____
5. look out _____

6. keep from _____
7. drop by _____
8. find out _____
9. sit back _____
10. see to _____

There is one piece of good news about phrasal verbs: some-times limited-English speakers who don't know the construc-tion can figure it out from the rest of the sentence, from what precedes and what comes after the verb. If you were to say, for example, "We will process your application as quickly as we can, but you can't count on it being ready before one week from now," the person you are speaking to would probably get the general idea that while their application might be ready sooner than one week, there is no guarantee. Be that as it may, if you had simply said "Don't expect it until one week from now," that would have been much clearer.

Phrasal verbs are one of the key differentiators that define limited English. They are learned some time after the funda-mentals, and their mastery is a reliable indicator that a person's English is no longer limited.

## 17. Don't use idioms.

Idioms are common expressions we use every day that pose the same problem for limited-English speakers as phrasal verbs do: you can know what each of the individual words in an idiom means and still not understand what the phrase means. Take a sim-ple example, *piece of cake*. Knowing *piece* and knowing *cake* doesn't do you any good because once again the parts simply don't add up to the whole. You either know what *piece of cake* means or you do not, but there's no way you're going to be able to figure it out. I once had an Indian friend say to me, "That's a piece of pie." I laughed, and then I realized what they had done: they had confused *piece of cake* with *easy as pie*. How odd it is that English has two idioms meaning simple or easy, and they both involve pastry.

Here are a few common idioms:

| | | |
|---|---|---|
| up in the air | cut corners | a stone's throw |
| take it easy | draw the line | a far cry from |
| out on a limb | lose your touch | sit on the fence |
| the last straw | see eye to eye | bend over backward |

You can see from this list that in some cases idioms are easier than phrasal verbs because there can be a relationship, however tenuous, between what the words mean and what the expression means. A person might be able to guess that *out on a limb* refers to a dangerous or precarious situation. Or they might be able to figure out that to *sit on the fence* means not putting your foot down on either side. Moreover, the individual may get considerable help from the rest of the sentence, from what precedes and follows the idiom. This is true for some idioms, but many others—*the last straw*, *up in the air*, *draw the line*—will always be elusive.

Once again, if you could rely on limited-English speakers to stop and ask you what the idiom you just used means, you wouldn't have to worry about using them, but that won't happen very often. So again the fix here is in your hands. The best advice is the same as it was for phrasal verbs: catch yourself in the act of using an idiom, stop, and rephrase.

This may be slightly easier to do in the case of idioms because somehow they draw a bit more attention to themselves than a phrasal verb. You can say *find out* almost without thinking (that's just the problem), but when you're in the middle of saying *out on a limb*, there may be a moment when you realize you're saying something a little odd. And of course there is always that helpful blank look that comes across the face of the other person when you use an idiom.

Appendix E has 60 common idioms. If you'd like to take a stab at (idiom alert) a bit of rephrasing right now, see if you can come up with substitute language for these 10 idioms.

1. up in the air _____
2. take it easy _____
3. lose your touch _____
4. the last straw _____
5. see eye to eye _____
6. bend over backward _____
7. a far cry from _____
8. at the drop of a hat _____
9. miss the boat _____
10. on the ball _____

*18. Use simple vocabulary.*

I almost did not include this piece of advice since it's so hard to describe what is meant by simple vocabulary, except perhaps through examples. In a general way, it means if there is an easy word you could use instead of a fancy or complicated one, then use it. Which of course only begs the question: what do you mean by easy, fancy, or complicated?

You could say ...

- *sign* instead of *indication*
- *help* instead of *assistance* or *aid* or *facilitate*
- *office* instead of *bureau* or *division* or *department*
- *person* instead of *individual*
- *pills* instead of *medication*
- *doctor* instead of *specialist*
- *come back later* instead of *reschedule*
- *we open (our door is open) at* ... instead of *our office hours are* ...
- *not able to* instead of *inability*
- *write your name* instead of *sign* or *signature*
- *like* instead of *prefer*
- *what would you like* instead of *what is your preference*
- *fill out again* instead of *resubmit* (although *fill out* is a phrasal verb)
- *easy for you* instead of *convenient*
- *choice* instead of *option*
- *begin* instead of *initiate*

It all depends on the situation, of course, but it might be useful if you and the other people in your office could sit down one day, at lunch perhaps, and brainstorm some of the most common words you use in speaking to your clients. Then decide which ones might be difficult for limited-English speakers and come up with more straightforward substitutes.

A friend of mine who used to work for the US Social Security Administration told me a story about a Vietnamese man who kept calling in to her office to ask for help. Several of my friend's colleagues spoke with the man, but he did not seem to understand them and kept calling back. Because my friend had lived in Laos, one of her colleagues asked her to listen in one day when the man called. The colleague told the man (I'm paraphrasing here): "Your payment authorization has to be signed off on by your department head and then forwarded to this division."

"I took the phone," my friend recalled. "And I told him: To get your money find the paper with the number 0818 in the bottom right corner. Take the paper to your boss. Tell your boss to write his name on the paper. Then take the paper and mail it to [and she gave the address]. Then your money will come."

One caveat about simple vocabulary: in the case of Spanish speakers, very often the fancy word—*indication*, *division*, *department*—is a cognate (see #19) and may be easier for the person to understand.

### 19. Become familiar with cognates; draw up a list.

A cognate is a word that exists in two or more languages and means the same thing but may be spelled and pronounced differently. Obviously, the two languages have to be related somehow or they wouldn't have any common words. One of the best-known cases of cognates occurs in the Romance languages, the language of the Romans: Latin. Officially, the Romance languages are Italian, French, Portuguese, Spanish, Romanian, and Catalan. While English derives from the Germanic branch of the Indo-European languages, especially its grammar and sentence structure, it is estimated that close to 50 percent of English vocabulary comes from Latin (or Greek), many words via French.

There are, accordingly, numerous cognates between English and the various Romance languages, especially between English and Spanish (as noted earlier); an estimated 35 percent of Spanish words, some 15,000, have English cognates. (See Appendix H for a few of the most common ones.) If we keep in mind that close to two-thirds (64 percent) of all limited-English speakers in the United States speak Spanish as their mother tongue, then the profusion of cognates is a godsend. Simply put, someone who speaks Spanish as their first language can potentially recognize over one-third of the most common English words.

But not if they don't hear them from you. If you tell a Spanish speaker that something is *up to* them, they won't have a clue. Or maybe you tell them it's their *choice* (*elección* in Spanish), and they will still struggle. But if you simply say *you decide*, they'll know immediately because *decide* is *decidir* in Spanish. If you explain to Carlos that *there are some difficulties* with his request, he may be confused (although difficult in Spanish—*difícil*—is somewhat close), but if you say there are problems (*problemas* in Spanish), he'll know right away what you mean. If you tell Maria the meeting has been *called off*, she will give you a blank look, but if you say it has been *canceled* (*cancelar* in Spanish), she'll understand.

Naturally, you'd have to know some Spanish (or other Romance language) to use cognates deliberately, so it might be a good idea to consult some websites or perhaps other staff members in your office who are familiar with Spanish. If there are certain words you use regularly in your job, you might draw up a list of any for which cognates could be substituted.

There are, in fact, a few rules which characterize many English-Spanish cognates, and if you're aware of these rules, you can use these words with some degree of certainty that they are cognates.

1. English words ending in *-tion*, such as *abstraction*, often have a cognate ending in *-ción*: *abstracción*.
2. English words ending in *-ary*, such as *secretary*, often have a cognate ending in *-ario*: *secretario*.
3. English adjectives ending in *-ic*, such as *classic*, often have a cognate ending in *-ico*: *clásico*.
4. English adjectives ending in *-ous,* such as *curious*, often have a cognate ending in *-oso*: *curioso*.
5. The English *-ct*—*conflict*—becomes *-cto* in Spanish: *conflicto*.
6. The English *-ly*—*completely*—becomes *-mente* in Spanish: *completamente*.
7. The English *-ty*—*variety*—becomes *-dad* in Spanish: *variedad*.

Finally, we would be remiss if we did not mention false cognates (also known as false friends), words which look almost identical in the two languages but have very different meanings and are thus not true cognates. A few common Spanish ones are:

- *reunión* which means *meeting*.
- *embarazada* which means *pregnant*.

- *actualmente* which means *currently*.
- *asistir* which means *to attend*.
- *decepción* which means *disappointment*.
- *éxito* which mean *success*.
- *idioma* which means *language*.
- *bizarro* which means *gallant*.
- *carpeta* which means *folder*.

It goes without saying that false cognates can get you into a lot of trouble. If there is a Spanish speaker in your office, you might want to ask that person to draw up a list of any common false friends that people in your job might use in everyday encounters. (See Appendix I for a list of 25 of the most common English-Spanish false friends.)

### 20. Write down words that appear difficult.

This is good advice no matter what, since people often recognize a word when they see it written but not when it is spoken, especially given the fact that English is not very phonetic. But it is an especially good idea in the case of a cognate or near cognate. If you're saying the word *difficult*, your interlocutor may not recognize it, but if you write it out, then a Spanish speaker will see the resemblance to *difícil* and understand you.

### 21. Avoid contractions, formal and informal.

**Formal** contractions take what are known as auxiliary verbs (*is, have, will, would*) and reduce them to a very brief sound attached to the preceding noun, usually a pronoun. As in:

- *He will* becomes *he'll*.
- *We would* becomes *we'd*.
- *I am* becomes *I'm*.
- *There is* becomes *there's*.
- *She is* becomes *she's*.
- *They will* becomes *they'll*.
- *We are* becomes *we're*.
- *The dog is lost* becomes *the dog's lost*.
- *What is important* becomes *what's important*.

By and large limited-English speakers need to hear all of a word, *any* word, not just a faint echo of it in order to grasp it. The auxiliary verb in a contraction goes by so fast and makes such minimal impact on the ear it might as well not be there. And if the person doesn't hear it, they don't know what you're saying.

If a person is not familiar with the contraction, then the sound it makes does not correspond to any English word; it's a nonsense syllable, in effect, and doesn't mean anything. Here are a few examples:

- I'm
- I've
- I'd
- you've
- he's
- she'll
- they've
- it'll
- they'll

Sometimes, however, the contraction does make the sound of a real English word and does mean something, but not in a way that's especially helpful. For example:

- *We'll* is something a car has four of.
- *He'll* is at the back of your foot.
- *We'd* is what you pull out of your garden.
- *We're* is the past tense of *was*.
- *We've* is how you make cloth on a loom.
- *I'll* is a row in a supermarket (or an island).
- *You'll* is Christmastime.
- *They're* could be *their* or *there*.
- *You're* could be *your*.

We should also throw the word *not* in here; it's not an auxiliary verb, but it shows up in numerous contractions: *can't, won't, didn't, shouldn't, isn't, aren't*. If the person doesn't know these contractions, then the sound they make conveys no meaning. For a more complete list of common contractions, see Appendix J.

Understanding contractions, like understanding phrasal verbs, is another sign that a person's English is becoming less limited.

You can only avoid contractions, of course, if you realize you're using them. So once again the task here is to listen to yourself and stop before you commit a contraction.

**Informal** contractions, words like *wanna* and *gotta*, are a close cousin of contractions but with one key difference. Contractions combine two words into one by leaving out one or two letters of the auxiliary word and retaining the rest. Thus *he will* becomes *he'll* by dropping the "w" and the "i" and retaining the two "l"s. But informal contractions, while also combining two words into one, replace the auxiliary word—typically *of*, *to*, or *have*—with something different altogether, usually with the letter "a."

You can see that while *he'll* bears at least some resemblance to its long form *he will*, *wanna* bears much less resemblance to its long form *want to*. Formal contractions are thus marginally easier for limited-English speakers to grasp than informal ones. Moreover, while a limited-English speaker could possibly have seen a contraction in its written form and thus be somewhat familiar with it (although not necessarily familiar with how it sounds when spoken), informal contractions are never written, except in fiction.

Thankfully, there are not nearly as many informal contractions as formal ones. Here are the 10 most common ones.

- *Could have* becomes *coulda*.
- *Going to* becomes *gonna*.
- *Got to* becomes *gotta*.
- *Has to* becomes *hasta*.
- *Lot of* becomes *lotta*.
- *Ought to* becomes *oughta*.
- *Out* of becomes *outa*.
- *Should have* becomes *shoulda*.
- *Want to* becomes *wanna*.
- *Would* have becomes *woulda*.

There are a few others (*kinda*, *sorta*, *dunno*), but these are much closer to slang and not used that often in public settings.

*22. Avoid special vocabulary: departmental, in-house,
job- or profession-specific language.*

Every government department, every occupation or profession, every job has its own special "insider" vocabulary. It's the way people talk to each other about what they do, but it's not something the general public is used to hearing, much less limited-English speakers.

- *provider* (as in health-care provider)
- *guest* (as in someone staying at a hotel)
- *agency*
- *shop* (as in our department)
- *disbursements*
- *assessments*
- *release* (as in release funds)
- *funds*
- *eligibility criteria*
- *balance* (as in bank balance)
- *facilities* (as in recreational facilities)

To put this advice into practice, you and your colleagues will first need to identify the most common insider vocabulary you use and then come up with replacements the general public will recognize. In doing this you might want to look at some of the literature (brochures, signs, instructions) your office produces; they often contain a lot of special, nonstandard vocabulary.

*23. Avoid slang.*

Slang is nonstandard English, actual words and phrases usually, but used in a way that is different from their standard or "real" meaning. Hence, when you use a slang word or expression, a limited-English speaker may know what the word means, the dictionary meaning, but not recognize what it means in its slang form. The individual may very well recognize the word *drunk*, for example, or *chicken*, but have no idea that they mean *intoxicated* and *coward*, respectively. Appendixes F and G contain a list of some of the most common American and British slang.

*24. Repeat what you said using different vocabulary.*

This advice comes next to last, but it's something you'll want to do right away if someone is having trouble understanding you. Let's say you've made one or more of the common mistakes described in this chapter, that you've used a phrasal verb, an idiom, a fancy word, a contraction, or some in-house vocabulary—and the person in front of you is clearly confused. Then the best thing you can do is to repeat what you just said *using different words*.

The beauty of this advice is that even if you don't know which part of what you said was confusing—if you're not aware, in other words, that you've used a phrasal verb or an idiom—as long as you don't repeat the same words, you may automatically correct the mistake you made without even knowing what it was. Moreover, when you repeat something, you will instinctively listen more closely to yourself since you now realize there was a problem with what you said (or you wouldn't need to repeat). Whenever you're paying conscious attention to your speech like that, you are much more likely to identify the problem and rephrase.

One caution here is that sometimes people want you to repeat because they didn't hear clearly what you said, not because they didn't understand it. In such cases, you should use the *same* words, not different ones.

### 25. Use the same words they use.

Once the conversation has begun and the other person has spoken, try to use the same vocabulary the limited-English speaker uses with you. These are obviously words they know, so you can't go wrong speaking their own English back to them. This will not always be possible, of course, such as when you have to change the subject, but when it is possible, it can be a very effective technique.

## Are You Serious?

While the whole idea in this chapter has been to inspire you with some sound advice, you could be forgiven for feeling a bit tired, overwhelmed, and maybe even depressed. You may be wondering, for example, how you can be expected to keep 10 different warnings in mind and still get out a single sentence. If I am so self-conscious and worried about making mistakes, I'll never be able to do my job. (And there's still another chapter, isn't there?) Help me understand how this has been good for me.

This is the problem with all self-help books; they contain so much advice, readers don't know where to start. Overwhelmed, they freeze and don't do anything. Only now they know they *should* do something—they've seen the error of their ways—so when they don't act after they've been "helped," they feel even worse about themselves than they did before.

Understood. But don't feel you have to master all the advice here at once, on multiple fronts, as it were. Pick one or two suggestions you think will be especially helpful or especially easy to carry out and just concentrate on those for now. Then you can add others later. Over time, almost all these techniques will become second nature, and you won't have to remind yourself to do them. If we left out sound advice simply for fear of overwhelming readers, then we'd be the ones deciding which pieces of advice are easiest or most helpful for you. But that's for you to decide.

And yes, you're right: there *is* another chapter still to come, six more in fact.

*Americans who travel abroad for the first time are often shocked to discover that despite all the progress that has been made in the past 30 years, many foreign people still speak in foreign languages.*

—Dave Barry
*Chicago Tribune*
Feb. 8, 1987

*Because I speak no Portuguese and have chosen to move through those parts of the city where tourists do not go, I find after a few days of not speaking that I have begun to doubt my own existence.*

—Moritz Thomsen
*The Saddest Pleasure*

# 6

# OTHER SPEAKING HABITS

*Later I asked him, "Was that Bengali you were talking?" Olly nodded. "I wanted to impress you." So then I asked him what he'd said to the official and he told me it was, "Yes, I quite agree, that is very true." So I asked what it was that the official had said to him first, and he roared with laughter and answered, "I don't know, I didn't understand a word!"*

—Christopher Isherwood
*A Meeting by the River*

Careful word choice on your part solves a multitude of challenges for limited-English speakers. If you did nothing more than monitor and adapt your vocabulary in the ways discussed in Chapter 5, you'd make limited-English speakers very happy—and yourself happy as well as you soak up their relief and bask in their appreciation.

If you're feeling that good, you might want to feel even better and consider a few more suggestions for helping these folks out. And the good news is that most of these remaining suggestions are either common sense, something you already know and may even practice, or very simple to implement.

## 26. Slow down!

This is advice most people are already aware of, probably because it's almost instinctive to slow down when you notice someone hasn't understood you. When you slow down, you make it possible for your interlocutor to hear every word you say. That doesn't guarantee they will know the words just because they hear them, but it's a sure bet that they will not know words they do not hear. Another advantage of slowing down is that you will automatically pronounce your words more clearly, a big plus for speakers of limited English.

Then there's the fact that when you speak more slowly, you automatically pay closer attention to what you're saying. And when that happens, suddenly all the advice from the previous chapter—all the talk about avoiding phrasal verbs, idioms, contractions—seems much more doable.

A final payoff is the appreciation limited-English speakers feel when native speakers slow down. They realize that you realize they are struggling, and they see that you're trying to do something to help them. Your solicitude comes as an enormous relief to them and eliminates a great deal of nervousness.

## 27. Don't raise your voice.

Sometimes we think people didn't understand us because they didn't hear what we said, so we raise our voice to solve the problem. While this may be the case and be appropriate in some situations, normally you and the other person are standing so close that you are bound to be audible. In that case, raising your voice has at least three unfortunate consequences that undermine the encounter.

To begin with, when you raise your voice people often interpret that as a sign that you are frustrated and getting impatient. And as we have seen multiple times, once limited-English speakers sense you're becoming annoyed, they become very agitated, and their grasp of English starts to slip away.

A second, equally unfortunate consequence of raising your voice is the embarrassment it causes the other person. Suddenly, what was a private or at least semi-private exchange has become very public and very humiliating. Any chance the person had of calming down and relaxing has just disappeared.

A final problem with raising your voice is the loss of good will it costs you. You may be seen as someone who doesn't have much self-control and is not very friendly, someone, in short, I'd rather not have to deal with today. And yet I have to.

### 28. Use shorter sentences.

You could say: "If you can complete that form and return it to me before 12 o'clock, when I go on my lunch break for one hour, then I can process it right away, and you won't have to wait around that long, but it's up to you."

Or you could say. "I am going to lunch at 12 o'clock. I will be back one hour after that. If you give me your application before I go, I can finish it quickly. Then you won't have to wait so long. It's your decision."

The two versions contain more or less the same words,

but the first version is one long sentence with five interlocking clauses. It's hard for limited-English speakers to absorb so much information in one spray of words, hard to know which part of this long sentence to pay the most attention to, and hard to know how the parts fit together. The second version is five separate sentences, with only one sentence containing a clause: "If you give me your application before I go, I can finish it quickly."

By and large simple sentences, those which do not contain introductory clauses ("If you can complete that form and return it to me"), parentheticals ("when I go on my lunch break for one hour"), and sentence extenders ("but it's up to you")—sentences without all these moving parts—are much easier on people with limited English; they don't have to figure out which parts relate to which other parts. When you say "but it's up to you" at the end of this long sentence, what chance does the individual have of knowing what part of the sentence that phrase refers to? (Not to mention that *up to you* is an idiom which probably means nothing to the person, and the word *process* is likewise probably a nonstarter.) To be sure we sometimes have to use compound sentences when we speak, sentences with a main clause and an additional, supporting clause or phrase; just try not to string too many of them together.

### 29. Use the active voice.

Here are two sentences:

1. That application form needs to be completed.
2. You need to complete that application form.

And two more:

1. That request can't be processed.
2. We can't process that request.

In each pair the first sentence is in the passive voice; no agent or doer of the action is specified, although it is understood to be *you* in the first pair and *we* or *your office* in the second pair. The second sentence in each pair is in the active voice; it names the agent (*You/We*) that is doing or not doing the action.

When we say that the agent is *understood* to be *you* (the limited-English speaker) in the first sentence and *we* (the office you work in) in the second, that's not quite true; that is only understood by a native speaker who is familiar with passive voice constructions. Because there is no agent named in passive voice sentences, you have to already know how these sentences work in order to figure them out. Passive voice sentences are difficult in many languages precisely because they require this kind of insider knowledge.

### 30. Use labeling language (metadiscourse).

You can say something. Or you can announce that you're going to say something and *then* say it. If you characterize what you're going to talk about before you start talking about it, this prepares listeners for what is coming. It doesn't mean they know what words you're going to use, unless you preview some of the words in your characterization, but at least they know what topic you're going to start talking about.

There is discourse, in other words, and there is meta-discourse. Discourse is talking, and metadiscourse is talk *about* the talking. Discourse is content; metadiscourse is commentary, description. Here are a few examples:

- You have three choices.
- Let me explain what that means.
- Let me make a suggestion.
- Now I will summarize how this works.
- The most important thing is...
- First, I want to talk about... and then we'll talk about...
- I'm going to say that again.
- Now I'm going to describe (talk about)...
- The biggest problem you will have is...
- The only thing you have to remember is...
- I'm going to ask you some questions.
- This next part is a little complicated.
- You need to listen very closely to...
- You need to understand three things.
- Let me repeat what I just said.
- Now I'm going to change the subject.

You get the idea. As long as you don't commit any word choice mistakes in your labeling preview, then telling listeners what they're going to hear next can greatly calm their anxiety. Moreover, if you use vocabulary in the metadiscourse that you're going to use in the discourse, that also helps listeners. In English we like to say *Get to the point*; here we're suggesting that you first preview the point and *then* get to it.

### 31. Don't assume people understood you; ask them.

It's only natural to assume that if people smile, nod their head, and don't ask you any questions, then they've understood what you're saying. We've already discussed smiling and nodding (Chapter 4), so we can start with what the absence of any questions tells you. The only thing it tells you for sure is that the person hasn't asked you any questions; what that means is another matter. In the case of limited-English speakers who are worried about taking too much of your time or otherwise upsetting you, it usually just means they don't want to take any more of your time or upset you any further, especially if there have been any difficulties thus far in the encounter. Their silence, in short, doesn't mean they don't have any questions; it just means they're not comfortable asking them. When you invite them to ask questions (see #32 and #33 below), they may be very relieved, and more to the point, they may get the clarification they needed so that now they do understand.

### 32. Don't ask: Do you understand? Do you have any questions?

So, by all means invite questions, but be careful how you do that. If you simply ask the person *Do you understand?*, there's a very good chance they will say yes whether or not they understood, for the reasons just described: fear of taking too much of your time or annoying you. And the same logic applies in the case of *Do you have any questions?*. The person may be very reluctant to say yes and prolong the encounter.

In both cases, the problem is that you've asked a yes/no

question in circumstances where the person may be very reluctant to say yes or no. So there has to be another way.

### 33. Ask open questions.

The solution here is to ask open questions, questions that cannot be answered with yes or no. Some examples include:

- What questions do you have?
- What would you like me to repeat?
- What part of what I said confused you?
- What can I explain again for you?
- Please tell me about anything you do not understand.
- How are you going to do what we just talked about?
- Can you explain to me what I told you?

### 34. Assure people it's okay to have questions.

When you ask your open question, you might preface it by assuring people that it's only natural that they will have questions, that you expect them to have questions, and that you will be disappointed if they don't ask you. *You must have questions*, you can say. *I will be happy to answer them. That's my job.* You might even tell them that almost everyone has questions so they shouldn't worry. This will go a long way toward mitigating any anxiety the person might have about taking too much of your time.

## Translation Frustration

Not all people who speak English as a second language will have to translate—out of and back into—English when they listen or speak to you, but most of them will, and especially those with limited English. The only ones who do not have to translate will be those who are bilingual.

So what happens during an exchange when the other person has to translate?

1. They hear you.
2. They translate your English into their mother tongue.
3. They think of their reply in their mother tongue.
4. They translate their reply into English.
5. And then they speak.

Notice that there are two additional steps here that the native speaker does not have to go through: translating from English into the mother tongue and translating out of the mother tongue back into English. We could say then that this process takes two-fifths or 40 percent longer than the conversation between two native speakers. That additional time has several consequences for you as the native-speaking interlocutor.

*35. Speak in shorter segments, thus pausing more often.*

If this is going to work for the limited-English speaker, you can't give them too many words all at once because they won't be able to remember that many when they start to translate. Speak one or maximum two brief sentences and then stop. And then after an interval (see below), you can speak additional sentences until you complete your statement. But the pauses are essential.

### 36. Wait twice as long for a reply as with a native speaker.

English speakers typically wait a maximum of three seconds for the other person to reply. After three seconds, we assume the person doesn't have anything to say, and we start speaking again. But if the person who has to translate takes 40 percent longer to complete the process and reply, then if you start up again after three seconds, that person is only halfway through the translation. When you pile it on like this, the person is going to give up quickly.

### 37. Let them know you know they have to translate.

This is critical. After all, the person knows they're taking longer than a native speaker and that this might annoy you, so they're already nervous. If you let them know that you know they have to translate, that you realize they're going to take longer than other customers, this can be an immense relief. And if they're relieved and calm, they can probably translate faster and reply sooner.

*I know your head aches. I know you're tired. I know your nerves are as raw as meat in a butcher's window. But think what you're trying to accomplish—just think what you're dealing with. The majesty and grandeur of*

*the English language; it's the greatest possession we have.*

—George Bernard Shaw

*English is the language of a people who have probably earned their reputation for perfidy and hypocrisy because their language itself is so flexible, so often light-headed with statements which appear to mean one thing one year and quite a different thing the next.*

—Paul Scott
*The Jewel in the Crown*

# 7

# THE TELEPHONE: A SPECIAL CASE

*Our language is funny: a "fat chance" and a "slim chance" mean the same thing.*

—J Gustav White

There is good news and bad news about the telephone. We will start with the bad news, so we can end on a positive note. Everyone recognizes that in many ways communicating with limited-English speakers on the telephone is harder than face to face. Nor is there any mystery about the main reason why: the other person can't see you and you can't see the other person. Let's consider the two halves of this dynamic in more detail.

## The Other Person Can't See You

It may seem counterintuitive to start with this half of the phenomenon; that's their problem, after all, not yours. Yours is that you can't see them. True enough, but the reader may by now have noticed that the vast majority of the suggestions in these pages derive directly from understanding how the spoken exchange is experienced by limited-English speakers; once you can see the dynamic from their perspective, see how it feels to them, then the things you can do to help become practically self-evident.

In this context, then, let's recall the very first point we made about talking with limited-English speakers, what is also one of the two or three most important lessons in this little book: you need to help them relax. That's the central theme of all the advice in Chapter 4: Staying Calm and likewise the logic behind the first two pieces of advice: #1 smile and #2 nod. These two pieces of advice come first for a good reason: they are two of the best ways to help limited-English speakers relax because they immediately signal that you are not frustrated, not in a hurry, and not agitated. This kind of nonverbal feedback from you is immensely reassuring and soothing to limited-English speakers; indeed, nonverbal cues like this are a key element in successful spoken exchanges between *any* two speakers. But in a phone call, they are not possible. If you consider, furthermore, how other types of even subtler body language—eye movement, how you hold your upper body (revealing tension or the lack thereof), even some small gestures—all send similarly soothing messages and how they are likewise not deployable during a phone call, then it's not hard to see how difficult, hence stressful, these conversations can be for speakers of limited English.

A closely related factor here is that when people can't see you, they can't tell if you understand what they are saying. Hence, they don't know whether they might need to repeat or perhaps rephrase what they said or in general how you are reacting to what they're saying—all of which can be very unsettling.

## *You Can't See the Other Person*

The other half of this dynamic complicates what is already a fraught exchange. When you can't see the limited-English speaker, you don't get any nonverbal cues that might tell you the person is having trouble understanding you, cues which would normally prompt you to slow down, for example, or to repeat something you said, or use a different choice of words. This might not matter that much if you could rely on the person to ask you to repeat or tell you they didn't understand, but for reasons we have already discussed, most limited-English speakers will not be comfortable doing that. It is true, however, that they might be less hesitant on a phone call when they have virtually no other way to let you know they can't understand you.

Pauses are another problem here. As we explained earlier, many people with limited English have to translate your words into and then back out of their native language before they can reply to you, and this takes approximately 40 percent longer than an exchange between two native speakers. As we said, most native English speakers normally wait a maximum of three seconds after they have said something to give the other person a chance to reply; if there is no response, we assume the person has understood or has no comment, and we go on to our next statement. If you can see the other person, you can often tell that they are processing your words and composing their answer, and you know enough to wait a little longer. When you can't see them, those two additional seconds of silence feel very awkward, and you may be inclined to start speaking before they've had a chance to finish translating.

We might also note here that not being able to see or be seen by the other person takes two additional strategies we present in these pages off the table:

> #12: Write down any words people are having trouble understanding.
> #49: Ask the person to write down any words you can't understand. (See Chapter 8.)

## Who's Calling?

We should also consider here why someone with limited English would even try to use the telephone to contact you in the first place and what it means when they do. Surely this person has had telephone conversations with native speakers before and has experienced how difficult they can be, especially as compared with face-to-face encounters which, challenging as they often are, are usually easier than phone calls. When a limited-English speaker calls you or your office, then, in most cases it's not because they prefer to use the telephone but because they're not in a position to come in and have to resort to a phone call. And that probably means the matter the person is calling about is somewhat urgent, something that can't wait until they have time to come in and talk to you. In other words, the person is probably nervous and anxious even before they pick up the phone, and if the conversation then starts to slip away—they can't understand you, you can't understand them—their anxiety increases and their English starts deteriorating on the spot.

And let's add one more consideration: if this individual knows that telephone calls are especially tricky, then they're not likely to place the call themselves if there is any way they can

find somebody else with better English to do it for them, someone in the household, perhaps, or a next-door neighbor, or even
someone they have specifically asked to come by today to help
them out in this situation. It's likely then, given these circumstances, that if they are calling themselves, it's not because they
want to; it's because they have to. Accordingly, whatever they're
calling about must be quite serious, and when the conversation
begins to unravel, their stress level is bound to shoot up, and
the chances of this conversation having a successful outcome go
from slim to none. (If you're not convinced about this, talk to a
911 operator.)

## What Can We Do?

In light of all the above, what can native speakers do to increase
the chances that telephone calls with limited-English speakers can have a successful outcome? While there are a handful
of strategies specific to phone calls (see #38–43 below), many
of the best strategies have already been described, including all those having to do with translation. The point to keep
in mind is that while these strategies are important to use in
face-to-face exchanges, they are essential to deploy during
phone conversations:

> #24: Repeat what you said using different vocabulary.
> #26: Slow down!
> #30: Use labeling language (metadiscourse).
> #35: Speak in shorter segments, thus pausing more often.
> #36: Wait twice as long for a reply as with a native speaker.
> #37: Let them know you know they have to translate.

#46: Ask the person to slow down. (People talk faster when they're under stress; see the next chapter.)

And here are six more strategies specific to phone calls.

### 38. Tell the person "You're doing fine."

When the other person can't see your reassuring nonverbal feedback (smiling, nodding) and therefore suspects or is worried you might be getting frustrated, you can let them know that's not the case by verbalizing that feedback. If you say things like *You're doing fine*, or *Don't worry, I'm going to help you*—the verbal equivalents of smiling and nodding—then you'll get the same results you'd get if they could see you.

### 39. Acknowledge that you know how hard this is for them.

This suggestion is closely related to #38. Limited-English speakers would not necessarily assume that you know that it's especially hard for them to conduct a conversation over the phone. If you can, reassure them in this regard—*I know this isn't easy. This is a little bit difficult, isn't it? This is always harder over the telephone*—they will appreciate your understanding and be greatly relieved.

### 40. Use Skype or Zoom when possible.

In some cases using Skype or Zoom might be an option. With Skype/Zoom, a telephone conversation is transformed into a very near equivalent of a live encounter, complete with the all-important, two-way nonverbal feedback, and you can apply most of the other suggestions we have made.

## If all else fails...

*41. Tell the person you will call back in X number of minutes during which time you will arrange for someone or some technology to be available to allow the conversation to proceed in the individual's first language.*

This strategy might not be possible in every case, but it should be possible in most cases. If the delay is reasonable, no more than 15–20 minutes, that should be enough time for you to still be able to help the person, even in most emergency situations.

## When You Call Them

The discussion so far has assumed that it is the limited-English speaker who is initiating the phone call, but in some cases, you are the one calling them. This changes the dynamic in some important ways. To begin with it means the person is caught off guard. Many limited-English speakers prepare to a certain extent when they make a phone call; they look up words they don't know and may even practice what they are going to say. Thus, they feel they have some control over the conversation, at least initially, and this may give them some confidence.

But when you call out of the blue, as it were, they are surprised and may even panic. Moreover, it means they don't have the chance to arrange beforehand for someone to be present who can help them.

*42. Ask the person if this is a good time to talk (when you initiate the call).*

One of the first things you should do when you reach the other person, before you launch into the reason for your call, is to ask the individual if this is a convenient time for them to talk to you. If it is, then obviously you will continue. If it's not...

*43. Offer to call back.*

Always offer the person the option of calling them back later when they can arrange for some help if they need it or just to give them time to calm down. Be sure to agree on the time you will call them back; if they are going to ask someone to be with them, that person may not be able to wait around indefinitely until you find the time to call again.

## The Good News

The above discussion notwithstanding, there is one important way that phone calls are less stressful, less anxiety-producing than face-to-face encounters, a factor that might make them more attractive to people with limited English and even make the exchange easier: phone calls are private and cause almost no embarrassment. After all, the person is not in a busy office, not standing in a line, not being overheard by a roomful of people, and in general is blissfully unaware of whether they're causing you any stress or frustrating anyone else. This takes almost all the humiliation and embarrassment out of the exchange, greatly reducing anxiety in the process, thus helping the person relax.

It doesn't make the challenges discussed above go away, but it does mitigate their effects.

*Why no "s" for two deer, but an "s" for two monkeys?*
*Brother Quang says no one knows. So much for rules!*
*Whoever invented English should be bitten by a snake.*
                                        —Thanhha Lai
                                 *Inside Out & Back Again*

*Despite the fact that English is the "international language," there is no denying that it is also a crazy language.*

*There is no egg in eggplant, nor is there any ham in hamburger. There is neither apple nor pine in pineapple. And while no one knows for sure what is in a hotdog, you can be pretty sure it isn't any kind of canine.*
                                        —Gayle Cotton
                             *Say Anything to Anyone Anywhere:*
                         *5 Keys to Cross-Cultural Communication*

# 8

# WHEN *YOU* CAN'T UNDERSTAND *THEM*

*They were under the impression that Arabic is the Brit-
ish language and were surprised when I told them we
had a language of our own.*

—Freya Stark
*The Valleys of the Assassins*

Thus far in these pages we have concentrated on what native speakers can do to make it easier for limited-English speakers to understand them. This is, after all, the part of the encounter that native speakers have control over and can do something about. But there is, of course, that other half of the conversation: the part where the limited-English speakers are talking and the native speakers are listening. There is no escaping the fact that what happens during this part of the exchange can complicate the encounter and jeopardize a successful outcome. If we have not addressed this issue, that's because at first glance there doesn't seem to be any way native speakers could influence what happens.

Be that as it may, it would be irresponsible not to at least acknowledge this dynamic and describe its effects. And, as it happens, it's not altogether true that we have not addressed this issue and that there is nothing native speakers can do about it.

We should begin by pointing out that it often comes as an unpleasant surprise to limited-English speakers that you might have trouble understanding them. As we mentioned in Chapter 3, this is your language they are speaking, after all, so why would you find it difficult? They get the point soon enough, of course, when the conversation goes nowhere, even though they may not understand why. Needless to say, it can be quite unsettling for them when they discover that on top of their not understanding you, you are also having trouble understanding them. If they were caught off guard by the first discovery, they are likely to be even more rattled by the second.

The chief effect of your not understanding their English is frustration, initially on your part but soon enough on the part of the limited-English speaker as well. It stands to reason that if you can't understand what your interlocutor is saying, either what questions they are asking or the answers they are giving to your questions, then you are going to be frustrated—regardless of whether you've done your best in your half of the conversation and the individual has in fact understood you. You will be frustrated primarily because the encounter is slipping away, but you may also be frustrated because the exchange is clearly going to be drawn out and time-consuming. Finally, you may be embarrassed, for yourself and perhaps even more so for your interlocuter, because while they are trying their best to speak your language, it's clearly not enough.

### 44. Try not to let your frustration show.

Whatever feelings you're having, your interlocuter is bound to be aware of them, especially any frustration. As soon as they pick up on your distress, they're going to be upset at not being able to make themselves understood and because of the trouble they know they're causing you. And as we have noted repeatedly elsewhere, when limited-English speakers become upset and agitated, they lose access to whatever English they know and the situation quickly deteriorates. We can see, then, that when you can't understand what a limited-English speaker is saying, as frustrating as that may be for you, it is often even more frustrating and upsetting for the limited-English speaker.

It's easy to say try not to let your frustration show, but it may be a bit harder to pull off. At the very least, try not to let it show in what you say to the individual, as you have some control over that. Don't say things like: *I'm having trouble understanding you. I didn't understand that. I don't know what you're saying.* The harder part of this is to somehow not let your frustration show in your body language, which tends to be automatic and unconscious and over which you thus have much less control.

### 45. Assume the blame.

It can be very reassuring to limited-English speakers to hear you say it's not their fault you don't understand them. It *is* their fault, of course, in the sense that they're the ones not speaking English very well, but they hardly need to be reminded of that. When you assume responsibility for not understanding them, they're not going to feel quite so bad about how an exchange is unfolding and may become more relaxed. Moreover, since they know it *is* their fault, they're going to immediately sense how kind you are to take the blame and realize they're dealing with a very sympathetic person. For limited-English speakers in acute distress, that can be very reassuring.

### 46. Ask the person to slow down.

When people are nervous, they often tend to speak faster than normal. But you need them to speak slower so you can clearly hear every word. You still may not recognize the words when you hear them but hearing them is the place to start. Here you might also practice suggestion #9, reassuring the person that you've got plenty of time and there's no need to hurry.

### 47. Try to isolate words you don't understand.

In many cases the reason you fail to understand what the limited-English speaker is saying is because of their accent. In short, the person is speaking English, using the right English words in the right places, but you just don't recognize the words. There are three possible reasons for this:

- The person is saying the correct English word but with, for example, a Spanish accent: saying *jess* for *yes*, *estop* instead of *stop*, *pool* instead of *pull*, *sheep* instead of *ship*.
- The person is saying the correct English word but putting the emphasis on the wrong syllable: saying *to<u>day</u>* instead of *to<u>day</u>*, *inter<u>est</u>ing* instead of *<u>in</u>teresting*, *ani-<u>mal</u>* instead of *<u>an</u>imal*, *tigh<u>ten</u>* instead of *<u>tigh</u>ten*.

- The person is substituting the native language word for a similar English word: saying *apartamento* instead of *apartment*, *atención* instead of *attention*, *nación* instead of *nation*. (Technically this is not an accent problem, but it's close enough.)

In most accent cases the task is to somehow pin down the word or words you're not recognizing. In an entire sentence or more, you probably recognize some or even most words, but there may be one or two key words that just aren't registering, and as a result the person isn't making any sense. If you can zero in on those words, you can at least locate the problem.

Don't forget, meanwhile, that many limited-English speakers are not aware that they speak English with an accent or, perhaps more accurately, do not realize you might have trouble understanding them. This is *your* language, after all, so why would you have any trouble understanding people speaking your mother tongue? Their surprise plus your confusion is an unfortunate combination.

### 48. Ask the person to repeat themselves.

Chances are you understand some of what the person is saying the first time they speak, but obviously not all of it. If you ask the person to repeat, they might use slightly different vocabulary, or slow down, or emphasize the important words, and these tactics may be enough for you to understand the second time. If it's not enough, at least you will have zeroed in on where the misunderstanding is happening and be able to work from there.

When you ask the person to repeat, you risk revealing that

you're struggling, hence making them nervous. But what other choice do you have? You might want to consider preceding your request by saying something like *Your English is very good, but I did not understand this one part*. Or *Please excuse me, but I did not hear you very well* (not strictly true but it doesn't cost you anything).

If you still can't figure out what the person is saying when they repeat, another good idea is to...

### 49. Ask the person to write down any words you can't understand.

If the problem is accent and you've isolated the problem word, this is practically a foolproof solution. You will almost certainly recognize the word when you see it written, even in those cases (*apartamento, atención*) when it's not exactly an English word.

### 50. Ask for help.

Sometimes nothing works. You've tried everything you can think of, and you still can't understand what the person is saying. But surely, you're not the only one in your office; perhaps there is someone else who is better at understanding people from certain countries or with certain accents. Ask that person to take over or, if they are not available, perhaps arrange for the limited-English speaker to come back later. This doesn't resolve the immediate problem, of course, but at least it gives the individual assurance that they can eventually get the help they have come for.

All the above suggestions will be helpful in the right circumstances, but we should add here that even if you do none of these things, you've already done the most important work by following the advice in the preceding three chapters. Why? Granted, that advice was not about how to understand limited-English speakers better but how to enable them to understand you better. But if you think about it, if they can understand you, if the conversation, against all their expectations, is going well, they're going to be very happy individuals. And not just happy but calm and relaxed, their anxieties greatly diminished. It's the best possible state for them to be in in terms of being able to access their English. If they still can't pull this conversation off, it won't be because you have not set them up for success.

*Fortunately, Caraka knew enough Aryan words to help me begin to comprehend not only a new language but a new world, for it is the language of a people that tells us most about what gods they worship and what sort of men they are or would like to be.*

—Gore Vidal
*Creation*

*If you don't [speak the language] you find yourself dependent on others to do even the most mundane tasks: post a letter, make a bank transfer, get a work permit, pay a bill. It can be very frustrating and quite demeaning, especially when you have to express yourself in the most simple terms as you haven't yet mastered the language.*

—Adrian Wallwork
*English for Interacting on Campus*

# 9

# CONVERSATION STYLE

*All over the world one can make oneself understood by gestures. But in India, impossible. You make a sign that you are in a hurry, that one must be quick, you wave an arm in a manner that the whole world understands, the whole world, but not the Hindu. He does not take it in. He is not even sure it is a gesture.*

—Henri Michaux
*A Barbarian in Asia*

There is an entire dimension of a face-to-face interaction that does not involve spoken language and therefore has not yet been addressed in these pages. This dimension, usually referred to as conversation style, involves a series of mostly nonverbal norms dictating how people are supposed to behave in a typical conversation. These norms differ significantly from culture to culture so that when two people with different norms interact, there is bound to be confusion and frustration. If native speakers are not aware of these cultural differences, they can easily misinterpret the behavior of limited-English speakers, and there's every chance one's own behavior will likewise be misinterpreted in turn.

I was once giving a workshop to an audience of language instructors at the Foreign Service Institute, the training division of the US Department of State. I asked an Israeli man, a Hebrew instructor, to describe typical Israeli conversation style. "We stand very close," he replied. "We look each other right in the eye. We talk very loudly. And we use lots of gestures."

Then I turned to a Japanese instructor and asked her to describe typical Japanese conversation style. "It's very easy," she answered. "It's the exact opposite of everything that man just said." And she went on to say that two Japanese people in conversation stand three feet apart, maintain limited eye contact, do not raise their voices, and use a minimal amount of gestures.

We will briefly consider six elements of conversational style below and describe how they can affect and in many cases disrupt a typical encounter:

- turn-taking
- eye contact
- personal space
- volume in speaking
- gestures
- facial expressions

## Turn-taking

When two people are in conversation, they have to take turns being the speaker and being the listener. Hence, there has to be a way for the speaker to signal to the listener that it's time to switch roles and for the listener to become the speaker. Different cultures do this differently, and these differences can seriously undermine the most common interactions.

In the United States and most other English-speaking countries, the way you signal to other people that it's their turn to speak is by pausing and saying nothing for approximately 2–3 seconds. That 2- or 3-second gap means: It's your turn. And if the listener wants to take a turn as speaker, they will start talking before the three seconds are up. If the person does not start speaking during that interval, the meaning is that they don't have anything to say at that point, and the original speaker can resume speaking.

In some other cultures—I have observed this in the Middle East, in the Mediterranean Basin, in India, and sometimes in Latin America—turn-taking is handled altogether differently. It works like this. The speaker begins; when it's time to give the listener a turn, the speaker repeats, summarizes, and generally recycles the point they've just been making. When the speakers start repeating themselves, *that's* the signal to the listener that I'm concluding now, so it's your turn to start, and the listener must start *before the speaker stops*. If the listener does not start, that's the signal to the speaker that the listener doesn't want to take a turn, and the speaker keeps on talking without stopping.

In this style of conversation, the listener must start speaking before the speaker concludes, which is the definition of an interruption in most English-speaking countries and is considered very rude. If you are in conversation with someone used to this pattern of turn-taking, this can raise havoc with the encounter in at least three ways:

- The person hears you repeat something, thinks you're signalling them to take their turn, and interrupts you.
- The person starts repeating themselves, signalling to you to take your turn; you wait politely until the person has stopped speaking; but the person doesn't stop because you have not interrupted, meaning you have nothing to say. In your mind the person monopolizes the conversation and never gives you a chance to say anything.
- You pause for 2–3 seconds to allow the other person to take their turn; they don't understand what this means (because they're waiting for you to signal them by repeating yourself); when they don't say anything after three seconds, you begin speaking again. In their mind you're rude because you never give them a chance to speak.

Notice another interesting effect of this difference in styles of turn-taking. In a culture where the listener must begin speaking before the speaker has stopped—where both people are briefly speaking at the same time—it would not make any sense to say anything important right up front because the first speaker is still talking and wouldn't hear it. Thus, the first thing the listener says would never be anything important because the other speaker isn't paying any attention yet.

Now think about English. We typically put the most important thing right up front, where speakers from some cultures never pay any attention. And similarly we listen very closely to the first thing other people say, where speakers from other cultures would never put anything important.

## Eye Contact

In most English-speaking countries, one of the ways people show they're paying attention is to maintain eye contact with the person who is speaking. People who don't maintain eye contact, then, aren't paying attention, and that's considered rude. But in many cultures, especially in the Asia-Pacific region, when an older person, a respected person, or someone in an authority position (that's you) is speaking, anything other than very brief eye contact with that person is considered disrespectful, impolite, and even challenging. Hence, many limited-English folks may look down when you're speaking to them to be polite and show respect. And you may interpret that as not paying attention, not being interested, or some other kind of rudeness.

In one study of behavior during negotiations, Americans maintained eye contact with their counterparts 30% of the time (which was also true for Germans and the British), while the rate for Japanese negotiators was 13%, or less than half as much time. In Brazil, long, sustained eye contact during conversation is preferred to intermittent contact, which often gets Brazilians accused of staring by people from Anglo-Saxon cultures (to say nothing of people from Japan).[1]

## Personal Space

Then there is the matter of personal space, specifically of how close two speakers stand in conversation in different cultures. The Anglo-Saxon norm is somewhere between 18 inches and 2 feet, meaning two people in conversation almost never stand closer than 18 inches or further than 2 feet. It has been said that if you extend your arm and make a fist, your fist should just touch the other person's shoulder blade.

Many parts of the world have a much closer norm, including India, the Middle East, the Mediterranean, sub-Saharan Africa, and parts of Asia and Latin America where, depending on the country, the norm is anywhere from 10–18 inches. Notice that the Anglo-Saxon minimum of 18 inches is the maximum in many cultures, whereas a merely average distance in some cultures, 12–14 inches, is 4–6 inches too close for many American and British people. The Japanese occupy the other extreme, trying initially to maintain 3 feet between themselves and the other person, perhaps because the Japanese bow when they meet.

How people from cultures whose norm is 12–14 inches behave can easily come across as aggressive to Anglo-Saxons; they are invading our space and perhaps even losing their self-control. Meanwhile, as we try to stand 2 feet away from people who consider 18 inches to be the maximum, we may come across as distant and unengaged.

## Volume in Speaking

Different cultures define "loud" differently. When someone from a culture with one definition speaks to someone from a culture with a different definition, each speaker is going to judge the other speaker's volume based on what their own culture considers loud.

The Anglo-Saxon version of loud, for example, is generally louder than the Japanese norm but somewhat softer than the norm for most Arabic-speaking countries. Thus, Americans and other Anglo-Saxons might wish the Japanese would speak up and that Egyptians would lower their voices. The Japanese, meanwhile, might wonder why Anglo-Saxons talk so loudly, while Egyptians might be put off by how softly we speak.

I use Egyptians as an example here because of a story an American woman told me in one of my workshops when we were talking about conversation style. She was from Minneapolis where she met and married her Egyptian husband when they were both studying at the University of Minnesota. She had never been to Egypt and never met his parents until they visited Cairo on their delayed honeymoon. After they had been at his parents' house a couple of days, this woman asked her husband why he had never told her that his parents didn't get along. When he asked what she meant, she asked him if he didn't hear them "fighting" in the morning at the breakfast table before she and her husband went down to eat. The woman did not speak Arabic and could not understand what her in-laws were saying, but they were talking so loudly she assumed they must be angry. He listened the next morning and said they were just talking about the weather.

In encounters between native and limited-English speakers, some of the latter might come across as aggressive or agitated if they speak louder than the Anglo-Saxon norm. Or they might be frustrated by how softly we Anglo-Saxons speak and not be able to hear us. If their English is limited, not clearly hearing every word we are saying can be a challenge; they at least need to hear the words, whether or not they recognize them.

## Gestures

In some cultures, people gesture a lot when they are talking, while in others, people use very few gestures. The Anglo-Saxon norm here is somewhere between the two extremes. We tend not to gesture as much as many folks do in the Middle East, for example, and even many Spanish speakers, but somewhat more than people from the Asia-Pacific region.

When someone gestures more than Anglo-Saxons do (and speaks louder), we often assume that person is getting a bit worked up, even upset, and we might become concerned and ask the individual to calm down. This, of course, will have the opposite effect on someone who is in fact behaving quite calmly by the norms of their culture but who now does indeed become agitated for being wrongly accused of acting upset.

Conversely, if we are dealing with someone from Vietnam, for example, compared with whom we use more gestures, that person may become nervous and agitated at how excited we've apparently become and even wonder if they have upset us.

While we're on the subject of gestures, much could be written (and has been) about how easy it is for two people to misinterpret each other's gestures if they come from different cultures. We can group the possible misinterpretations into three categories:

- A gesture that means one thing in one culture and something very different in another culture. This is the worst case of gesture confusion. The Anglo-Saxon gesture for go away, for example—hand out, palm down, bringing the fingers in—is the gesture for come here in some cultures. When both cultures have the same gesture but it means something different, the result is you send message A and the other person interprets it as message B, and vice versa. The American gesture for okay, to use another example, the thumb and index finger forming a circle, is an obscene gesture in some other cultures.

- A gesture that means something in your culture and means nothing (is not a gesture) in another culture. The result here is that you think you've sent a message, but none has been received.

- A gesture that means something in another culture but means nothing (is not a gesture) in your culture. The result here is that limited-English speakers think they have sent you a message, but you haven't received it.

It's easy to see how gesture differences can add to the confusion of a typical encounter between people from two different cultures.

## Facial Expressions

The degree of animation, of how much facial expressions reveal emotions, also differs from culture to culture. In many cultures in the Pacific Rim, especially Southeast Asia, people have what is known as a low affect, meaning they do not let their inner feelings show in facial expressions, gestures, or speaking volume. People from western countries who try to read meaning into each other's facial expressions struggle with many Asians because there's nothing to read. Some Asians, of course, might be alarmed or even embarrassed at how *much* there is to read in the facial expressions of many westerners.

I once gave a cross-cultural workshop to a group of Vietnamese folks in Boston, and I was sure the session had bombed because their faces remained impassive throughout the workshop.

Much to my surprise, several participants came up to me after the presentation to tell me how much they enjoyed it.

Many observers have noted that in the Middle East, the Mediterranean, and much of Latin America people are more ani- mated in conversation than folks in North America and north- ern Europe. They may interpret North Americans, therefore, as being a bit disengaged and uninterested, and North Americans may worry at how excited these folks are becoming.

## The Mehrabian Study

If you've read this far in this chapter, you will probably not be surprised at the results of a famous study Albert Mehrabian did (in the United States) of the three elements that comprise what he called the "total meaning of a spoken message" when two people are face to face.[2] The elements and the percentage of the meaning each contains are as follows:

| | |
|---|---|
| Linguistic content (the meaning of the words) accounts for | 7% |
| How you say the words (intonation, volume, speed) accounts for | 38% |
| Nonverbal communication (facial expressions, gestures, body language) accounts for | 55% |

Note that four of our six conversation style elements fall into Mehrabian's nonverbal category, which on its own contains *over half* the meaning of a spoken message. If you misread close to half the content of a spoken message or if a limited-English speaker misinterprets nearly half of your content, the result, whatever else it might be, could hardly be called successful communication.

## The Perfect Storm

Each of the elements of conversation style on its own is a likely cause of cross-cultural misunderstanding, but when the six elements are combined, they can easily create a perfect storm of confusion and misinterpretation. A "loud" Arabic speaker, making a bit "too much" eye contact, standing a "mere" 12 inches away, using "lots" of gestures, with "very animated" facial expressions, and to all appearances "monopolizing" the conversation... well, you can finish the sentence.

As someone in a public-facing position, if you are aware of these conversation-style differences, then you will be less likely to misinterpret some of the behaviors you may encounter. And you will also be in a better position to understand how some of your own behaviors are being perceived and quite possibly misinterpreted by others. This kind of awareness, in short, will sometimes help explain behaviors and reactions to your behavior that otherwise make no sense.

*Really, it is unfair to say that English spelling is not an accurate rendering of speech. It is—it's only that it renders the speech of the 16th century.*

—Guy Deutscher
*The Unfolding Language: An Evolutionary Tour of Mankind's Greatest Invention*

*And then of course your sentences, intended with just the shade of meaning you desire, come out shorn of all accessories, quite useless for anything except the mere procuring of bread and butter.*

—Freya Stark
*The Journey's Echo*

# SPECIAL TOPICS

*Hindi is spare and beautiful. In it we can think thoughts that have the merit of simplicity and truth and convey these thoughts in correspondingly spare, simple, truthful images. English is not spare. It cannot be called truthful because its subtleties are infinite. It is the language of a people who have probably earned their reputation for perfidy and hypocrisy because their language itself is so flexible, so light-headed.*

—Paul Scott
*The Jewel in the Crown*

This chapter deals with several topics that don't lend themselves to specific pieces of advice, but which directly impact the native/limited-English speaker encounter. As such, these are phenomena that public-facing individuals have to deal with and could benefit from knowing about.

## Line? What Line?

For reasons beyond the scope of this book, many immigrants come from cultures where the habit of queuing, of standing in a line to wait for a service, is not as common as it is in most English-speaking countries. To be precise, it is the habit of being waited on *one at a time* that is not well understood or widely practiced. Accordingly, in place of a line in these cultures you often find a knot of people arrayed in a semi-circle in front of the service provider, several people vying for—and receiving—the provider's attention *at the same time*. Whether or not this happens depends entirely on circumstances, as even in countries where lines are less common, people do line up in some places, such as banks.

Immigrants from some of these cultures may not understand that you cannot serve more than one person at a time and they may cut in line, coming straight up to you and trying to get your attention while you are serving the first person in line. Naturally, you, to say nothing of the other people in line, will find this behavior annoying and rude, and you will need to address it—or the others will do it for you. Remember, though, that the person is probably already nervous just being in that setting; if you can quietly explain the lining-up protocol, minimizing any embarrassment, you will do the individual a great kindness.

## Being Late for Appointments

Many of the same people who don't understand the logic of lines likewise have a casual attitude toward time and appointments (from an Anglo-Saxon perspective, anyway). In some of their home countries being "on time" means being up to as many as

30 minutes late from the perspective of a more time-conscious culture. In the United States and most other English-speaking countries, even five minutes is considered late; it's normal, in fact, to arrive a few minutes before an appointment.

If your job involves making appointments for members of the public or even just for the individual to come back and see you at a later time, you should not assume the person realizes that anything over five minutes is unacceptable. You must explain that if they come five minutes late, they will be asked to come back again at a later date.

## Indians: A Special Case

As of 2015, somewhere between 3 million and 3.4 million Indian Americans, defined as anyone whose ancestry can be traced back to an ethnic group in the country of India, lived in the United States, comprising 1 percent of the total US population. The three states containing the most Indians were California (19 percent of the total), New Jersey (11 percent), and Texas (9 percent). The five US cities with the most Indian residents were New York City, Chicago, Washington, DC and suburbs, Los Angeles, and San Francisco.[1]

In the UK there are close to 1.5 million Indians, making them the single largest ethnic minority.[2] Many of them, of course, are second or third generation and have never lived in or perhaps even visited India. A recent *Forbes* report found that the number of Indians who became permanent residents in Canada increased from 39,340 in 2016 to 80,685 in 2019, an increase of more than 105 percent.[3] In Australia there are over 700,000 Indians, and their numbers are expected to overtake those of Chinese-born Australians in this decade.[4]

The vast majority of Indians living in English-speaking countries are either bilingual or certainly speak English very well, to use the American Community Survey terminology. As someone in a public-facing job, you're not going to meet very many Indians who have any trouble understanding you. So how do they end up in a book about limited-English speakers?

## Fast Talkers

They may not have trouble understanding you, but you may have trouble understanding them. The main problem you will experience is that many Indians talk extremely fast, especially those who come from a southern Indian background. The Dravidian languages spoken in southern India—Tamil, Telugu, Kannada, and Malayalam—are among the world's fastest languages. When a native speaker of one of those languages is speaking in their mother tongue, they are speaking faster than almost anyone else in the world. (Tamil is reportedly the fastest of the four.)

The problem arises when these folks switch to English to talk to anyone who doesn't speak a Dravidian language, including most Indians in the rest of the country—and to you. Because they speak so fast in their mother tongue, their natural tendency is to speak English equally fast, and that is too fast for most native-English speakers. Indeed, it's even too fast for most other Indians; I've frequently heard northern Indians (who typically do not speak any Dravidian-derived language) ask southern Indians to slow down when they speak English. The new-employee orientation manuals of many of the large Indian outsourcing giants—Tata, Wipro, Cognizant, Infosys—warn new hires to slow down when speaking to their western clients. In a multi-year survey I took for a large North American Fortune 500 business services company, American employees listed the inability to understand Indians on the telephone as one of their biggest challenges working with folks from India.

If you are speaking with someone whose mother tongue is one of these four Dravidian languages, you may very well have to ask them to slow down. And even then, they may slow down for a sentence or two and then revert to form. So you'll have to ask again. Don't be embarrassed or feel awkward—it's not you, they really are talking fast.

Some readers may interact a lot with Indians, in person (as colleagues) or on the phone with offshore Indian service providers, and you may want to or even need to get better at understanding them. One thing you can do is to rent English-language Indian movies, movies with Indian actors who are all speaking English to each other. These would either be movies made for a worldwide audience or, in some cases, movies made for distribution inside India for the large English-speaking population. Some examples are *Slumdog Millionaire, Monsoon Wedding, The Lunchbox*, and *The Namesake*.

The beauty of renting these movies (other than the fact that many of them are terrific movies) is that you can listen to English being spoken by Indians but you don't have to understand, don't have to respond, and you can rewind and play passages over and over. Remember, though, we are talking about *English-language* Indian movies, not Hindi movies.

We might add a note here concerning the strategy many folks use when they can't understand Indians on the telephone, especially Indians with whom they work in any kind of offshore partnership. The natural instinct in these cases is to adopt the all-email approach, conducting as much business as possible entirely in writing. It makes perfect sense: if understanding Indian speech is the problem, then take the communication out of the realm of speech.

That can certainly be justified in several situations, but it is something of a trade-off: while you will understand what the person is saying when you read it in an email, you will at the same time be minimizing your exposure to Indian speech. If all your interactions with Indian colleagues can be carried out exclusively in writing, then minimizing your exposure is fine. But if some of them still require talking on the phone from time to time, then the only way you're going to get better at understanding Indian speech is to increase—not decrease—your exposure to it.

## Indian English

Another challenge you may face with Indians is their use of Indian English. For the most part Indian English is like American English and even more like British English. But there are several words that exist in both standard and Indian English but which mean something very different. You will recognize these words, in short, and you will likewise assume you know what the person is saying, but you will be mistaken. And Indians, of course, will assume you attach the same meaning to these words as they do, that they understand you, and they will likewise be mistaken.

A list of some of the most common words and expressions is in Appendix K, but here are a few by way of illustration:

| Word | Standard English meaning | Indian English meaning |
|---|---|---|
| revert | go back to | reply or respond |
| gum | chewing gum | glue |
| cabin | a small hut or dwelling | an office or cubicle |
| intimate (verb) | suggest or imply | inform or notify |
| fresher | the comparative form of *fresh* | a new hire |

These words are all widely used and readily understood by other Indians, of course, so it will come as a surprise to a lot of Indians when you don't understand them or misinterpret what they mean.

We might digress briefly to talk about one particular example of Indian English that often comes up in the kind of encounters we are describing in these pages: the word *doubt*, as in the common Indian expression *I have a doubt*. Indians use this expression to mean *I have a question*, but although they certainly know the word *question*, they deliberately choose to replace it with *doubt* because to Indians the word *doubt* sounds more polite in this context. Ironically, choosing to say *doubt* in place of *question* sounds less polite to native English speakers, as we'll explain in a moment.

Back to *doubt*. Why do Indians think it's more polite to say *I have a doubt* instead of *I have a question* when they don't understand something? The way it was explained to me is that if you say you have a question to someone, the meaning is that person did not explain something very well and they are the reason you did not understand. And that's rude. But if you say, for example, *I have a doubt* to Anna, that means you doubt your ability to understand Anna's excellent explanation and you are the reason you did not understand. And that's polite.

Ironically, it's much more polite in America and other English-speaking countries to tell someone you have a question rather than a doubt because the latter means you don't believe something the person said. The bottom line is just to keep in mind that if you do explain something to someone from India and they tell you they have a doubt, it just means they have a question. They're not saying they don't believe you.

## Accent? What Accent?

It's also going to be news to many Indians that they speak English with an accent. No one ever accused them of this before they left India, of course, because the people they were speaking to were other Indians who spoke English with the same or a very similar accent. Even if fast-talking Indians slow down when you ask them to, you may still have trouble understanding them because of their accent, and you will have to ask them to repeat.

## I Never Had Any Problems Before

Your interactions with Indians are further complicated by the fact that for many Indian immigrants this is the first time in their lives that anyone has ever had any trouble understanding them when they speak English. And that's because up until the time they left India, they had been speaking English mainly or even exclusively *to other Indians*. Other Indians, that is, who may talk as fast as they do, who use the same Indian English words, and who have a similar accent. Of course they understood each other.

People who have been speaking English successfully all their life are going to find it very hard to believe they're not making themselves understood. And they are quite likely to assume this is your fault, not theirs. Hence, they often become frustrated, indignant, even insulted when you can't understand them or when you ask them to repeat. Try not to react; that won't help.

*The English language is like London: proudly barbaric yet deeply civilized, too, common yet royal, vulgar yet processional, sacred yet profane.*

—Stephen Fry
*The Ode Less Travelled*

*[A middle-class Englishman] is very suspicious of foreigners, chiefly on the grounds that they do not have baths, disguise their food with odd sauces, are oppressed by their rulers and priests, are dishonest, immoral, and dangerous, and talk a language no one can make head or tail of.*

—Alec Waugh
*Labels*

# HOW LIMITED-ENGLISH SPEAKERS CAN HELP THEMSELVES

*There is nothing intrinsic in the English language that made it attain such prominence. It is far from easy to learn. (A recent study found that it takes much longer for an infant to learn English than, for example, Spanish; the world would indeed have been better off if Spanish had become the universal language.)*

—Minae Mizumura
*The Fall of English in the Age of English*

**B**efore you ask, the answer is no. As in no, we're not expecting people with limited English to be reading this book. How could they? And you probably have a follow-up: so why is there a chapter here telling those folks how they can improve their English?

Part of the answer is because there are many ways limited-English speakers could easily improve their English *if they could just be made aware of them.* The rest of the answer is: you *are* reading this chapter, and with very little effort you could become the means whereby the advice herein reaches and greatly benefits people with limited English.

But wouldn't I have to be bilingual to do that? I'd have to be able to translate, right? Yes, you would, and if you're not bilingual, that does present a problem. But not much of a one: if you're not bilingual yourself, you must know someone who is. And if you don't know anyone who is, then surely someone you know knows someone who is. At the end of the day, there are a lot of bilingual folks out there, especially Spanish speakers (in the United States), with good English. If the information in this chapter can get into the hands of bilingual folks, then sooner or later it can reach people with limited English.

We did hesitate as to whether to include this chapter or not, but in the end, it seems likely that anyone who gets this far in these pages is someone who wants to help people with limited English. Why else would you have stayed with us for 10 chapters? We'll leave the details to you and your friends, but if you're at all willing to alert a few bilingual folks to the existence and the content of this chapter, some of them will be willing to do the rest and pass this advice on. In the process you will be instrumental, directly or indirectly, in helping transform the lives of many people for the better.

So yes: this book has been written for *you*, for native speakers of English, to help you enable limited-English speakers to understand you better. And that takes care of one half of the encounter quite nicely: the half when you are speaking. But it doesn't address the other half, the part when the limited-English folks are speaking. Just think, though, how much more efficient it would be if this problem could be attacked from both ends simultaneously: you work on how to make yourself better understood, and the limited-English folks work on how to understand you better. We've spent 10 chapters covering the first topic and its audience, now it's time to address the second one and its audience.

## NOTE TO NATIVE SPEAKERS: CONSIDER READING THIS CHAPTER YOURSELF

One more thing: you might construe all the above to mean you can skip this chapter as long as you make sure it gets into the hands of bilingual types. And that's perfectly fine. Well done! But we would humbly suggest you might want to take a few minutes (you'll need approximately 18 of them to be precise; we timed it) and read the chapter yourself. To be sure, it was written expressly for and is addressed to folks with limited English, but native speakers will glean many insights from this chapter into the world and the everyday reality of immigrants and other limited-English speakers. And you will also understand why we made some of the suggestions that appear in the rest of Part 2. Those 18 minutes, in short, will be richly rewarded.

Our advice here will come in two batches: ways limited-English folks can increase their exposure to English and ways they can increase their use of English. We will start with the former as these are suggestions that are not only easy to put into practice but that are also not likely to frighten away anyone with limited English.

## Increase Your Exposure to English

Among the easiest and least threatening ways for limited-English speakers to improve their English is to put themselves in situations where they can hear native speakers talking *but do not have to respond to them.* Not having to respond means they don't have to understand what's being said, creating an ideal situation where limited-English speakers can relax completely and simply absorb the sounds of English. This isn't the same as speaking, of course, but mere exposure to a spoken language is the single best way to learn how to speak it. This is exactly how young children learn their mother tongue, after all, by hearing it spoken by their parents, older siblings, cartoon characters on TV, and others. If it works for native speakers, it should work for anyone with limited English.

### 1. Sit next to native speakers on the bus or the train.

Needless to say, you can't just walk up to two people talking and ask them if you can listen to them. ("You" will be used from this point forward to refer to those with limited English.) But there are many circumstances where you will just naturally be close enough to two people speaking English to be able to overhear them. If you use public transportation, try to sit near other people and not by yourself somewhere. If no one near you is talking, can you move closer to where two people are talking?

### 2. Frequent public places where you're going to hear English.

Make smart choices. You can always get your hair cut at a hair salon or barbershop where everyone speaks Spanish. Or you could go to a place where only English is spoken and where you will be forced to speak it, too. You could have your car serviced at a garage where everyone speaks your mother tongue or where the mechanics all speak English—and where you'll have to try your best. You can frequent a restaurant where all you will hear will be your first language or you can eat in a place where everyone speaks English and get some practice. And in a place where they do speak English, you can either sit at a table or in a booth quite far from other customers, or you can sit close enough to overhear their English and improve yours just by listening.

### 3. Watch television shows, including children's shows, and go to movies in English.

You can watch television or go to the movies for two reasons: to relax and enjoy the show or to improve your English. For the former, all you need to do is find a TV station or streaming service that carries programs in your mother tongue or go to a movie in your first language. But when you're watching TV to improve your English, listen to any of the many English stations on your television or computer or go to one of the many local cinemas.

Any TV show or movie will suffice, but you might want to consider watching at least a few children's shows and going to animated movies aimed at younger audiences. Most public television stations in the English-speaking world have an entire channel devoted to children's shows. The English used in these shows will always be simpler than that used in TV shows and movies intended for adults. And don't forget that watching children's television shows is how all those native speakers first learned their English. As noted earlier, if it's good enough for native speakers, it's good enough for you. If you have children, it will be especially enjoyable to watch these shows along with them.

Sometimes at the end of a long day, the last thing you will feel like doing is improving your English; you just want to sit in front of the TV and relax. But there may be some days, such as on the weekend when you're not so tired or so busy, when you say to yourself: I'm going to spend 30 minutes today working on my English. And all you have to do is sit down and turn on the television. Remember: you don't have to understand a word of what's being said; you just need to be exposed to the language.

### 4. Rent movies in your mother tongue with English subtitles.

This is going one step further than mere exposure, this is hearing English and having it translated—exposure with comprehension. It doesn't get any better than that for trying to improve your English.

### 5. Listen to the radio.

If you have a car, turn on the radio, listen to an all-English station, and soak up the language. The number of words per minute you will hear on the radio is greater than via any other single means; it is exposure par excellence. And you don't have to understand a single word.

*6. Read things written in English.*

This is not the same as hearing English, of course, the common element in the first five suggestions, but it is like them in the sense that it is completely nonthreatening; you do it on your own terms, whenever you feel like it, for as long as you like, and you don't have to understand or respond to what you are reading.

You can read anything, of course, but you might want to start with something simple, anything written for young children, including anything with pictures. If you happen to have small children of your own or someone else in your family or your circle of friends does, then reading these books to them can be especially fun and rewarding. You can also try books written for older children and for young adults. And there are newspapers, magazines, and all kinds of online publications to choose from.

*7. Listen to audio books while following along with the written version.*

Many books have been released in an audio version, with someone reading the text out loud. If you buy the book and then listen to the audio version while following along on the page, you will not only hear English being spoken (more exposure), but you will see how the written words are pronounced. And you can stop anywhere you want if you need to hear something repeated by the reader.

## Increase Your Use of English

All the above suggestions will be immensely helpful, laying the essential foundation for acquiring English. But you can't just listen to English; sooner or later you'll have to begin speaking it.

### 8. Attend a language class.

These days there are at least two ways to take a language class: you can register for an actual class and show up in person at the class location. Or you can take an electronic version of a class, something online perhaps, or audio programs you buy and listen to on headphones, or some kind of language app you can download and follow on your phone, your tablet, or some other device. And you can easily do both. We will discuss the first option here and the electronic version in our next section.

Attending a language class is probably the easiest way to begin the transition from listening to English to speaking it. Why? Because a language class is a nonthreatening environment in which to practice speaking. It is an artificial environment, after all; nothing you say in a classroom really matters. If you make a mistake or don't understand something, there are no consequences. And if you make a fool of yourself, you don't feel embarrassed because everyone else is doing the same thing. Finally, when you see that other people speak English at your level, make many of the same mistakes, and otherwise struggle with English just as much as you do, you will feel much better about yourself. Attending a language class in person is not just a way to learn and practice English, it's also a way to learn that you are not alone.

But attending a language class is not always easy. Many people only have time for a language class at the end of the day, after work. But after work and commuting, you may be very tired; even if you feel like taking a class, you might not be able to concentrate or learn very much. One suggestion here is not to sign up for a class that meets every evening, maybe just two or maximum three times a week. Or perhaps a class that meets on the weekend when you have more free time and are not so tired from work. Also try to find a class as close to your home as possible so it doesn't take long to get there and so you don't get home too late after the class.

When you are thinking about taking a class, be sure to get advice from other people you know who have attended classes. They had many of the same questions you have, and they had to overcome many of the same obstacles. Other people were nervous and did not want to do this for the same reasons you are nervous and do not want to do it. But they did it anyway. Ask them how.

### 9. Study and practice English on your own with language apps and online learning programs.

Attending a language class in person may be difficult for reasons we have described above: the location may be inconvenient, the times of the class may be inconvenient, you may be too tired at the end of the day to attend a class. Despite these problems, we strongly encourage you to sign up for a class, for several reasons:

- You will meet other people like yourself and realize you are not the only one struggling with English.

- You may get valuable suggestions from others on how to improve your English.
- You will become part of a mutual support group, encouraging and inspiring each other to persevere in your efforts.

But in addition to attending a class, even if only once or twice a week, you can pursue your study of English on your own, at your own pace, on your schedule, and without having to leave home. There are many language applications you can purchase and download to various electronic devices. You can also attend classes online, either live classes or classes you purchase and then click on and follow any time you want, repeating lessons or parts of lessons over and over. And you can even listen to language classes on your headphones when you are taking a walk or commuting, or listen through your car's audio system when you are driving to the grocery store or to church.

We recommend a combination of #8 and #9. Attending a class offers important benefits you can't get by studying on your own. But self-study is no doubt easier and more convenient for many people, and it can supplement and support what you learn in an in-person class.

### 10. Speak in English to other people who speak your first language.

This advice may sound odd. Why would you talk in English to someone who speaks your own first language, especially if you do not speak English very well? The answer is simple: to practice. To be sure, most of the time when you talk to your friends, you are...well...talking: exchanging information, news, opinions—whatever people talk about in everyday conversation. But sometimes you might try talking just to practice speaking English. You can still talk about the same things, but you have a second agenda: to improve your language skills.

This will probably feel awkward, but if you remember you are doing this deliberately to develop your English, then you can both laugh and try it for a little while. And that's important: to only do it for 20 minutes or half an hour, because you may get tired.

The great advantage of this suggestion is that it is not threatening, embarrassing, or stressful speaking English to close friends the way it is to native speakers whom you may not know very well or not know at all. With friends, it's not serious and you can relax; there are no consequences if you make mistakes or if you don't understand the other person. No one gets frustrated or upset. And if your friend speaks English better than you do, then you can learn from them. Or vice versa.

## 11. Put yourself in situations where you have to speak English.

When you are just learning English, some English-only environments can be very threatening, situations where you may become quite agitated if you can't understand what's being said. But there are some English-only environments—the grocery store, a barbershop, a restaurant—where your limited English is not a serious problem with serious consequences. These are good places for you to practice your English without having to worry if you can't understand or can't make yourself understood. So sometimes have a nice relaxing meal at your local *cafetería*, but other times be brave and go to a place where no one understands Spanish.

## When You Can't Understand What Native Speakers Are Saying

Your biggest fear as someone who speaks limited English is to be in situations where you can't understand what a native speaker is saying. This is completely normal, of course, but it can be very stressful—and even cause you to forget what little English you may know. Moreover, you will also be worried that you might upset or annoy the native speaker and that you are taking too much of their time. And this only makes you more nervous. Here is some advice for these situations.

### 12. Remember: most native speakers just want to help.

It depends on the circumstances, of course, but in many cases the people you are speaking to will be sympathetic, especially if they work in a service position where their job is to help members of the public. They have had to speak to people with limited English many times before, and they understand your situation. As a result, these people will not easily become annoyed or frustrated with you, and they already know it may take more time to help you than it does to help other people. So you should not worry too much about bothering them.

### 13. If you don't understand something, you must let native speakers know.

You must be sure to tell someone that you have not understood what they just said. While you may naturally be reluctant to do this, for the reasons we just discussed above, how can people know you did not understand them if you don't tell them? And remember: they may be much more sympathetic and understanding than you expect.

### 14. If a native speaker asks, Did you understand?, do not say yes if the answer is no.

You may feel that if you tell a native speaker you did not understand them, the person may become frustrated and upset with you. To begin with, this is not necessarily true: the person wants to help and if they know you did not understand, they will explain again. And even if it is true, even if they do become frustrated, isn't it better if you can understand them? If you don't understand them and don't tell them, you may do something wrong, and then they will be even more upset with you! To be sure, some days you will decide it's just not worth it to upset people, but on other occasions you can't worry about that; you have to get the job done no matter what.

### 15. If a native speaker asks, Do you have any questions?, don't say no if the answer is yes.

Sometimes you may hesitate to admit that you have questions. But if you do have questions, how can you get answers if you don't ask them? Don't forget: the person wants to help. But how can they help if they don't know what you need?

## A Word to Those Who Live in an Immigrant Subculture

Some of you may live in a place where there are many other people from your home country or if not from the same country, then at least other people who speak your mother tongue. You can go about many of your daily activities without ever meeting or talking to anyone who speaks only English. You may even be able to find work in an environment where everyone speaks your first language.

Such a subculture is very comforting and supportive when you arrive in your adopted country, especially when you are going through culture shock, that period of transition when you miss many things and many people from your home country, perhaps even close family members you have left behind, and have to learn all the new ways of doing things in the new country. All these adjustments can be overwhelming, so it can be extremely appealing to spend time in an environment that is familiar and reminds you of home—and where you don't have to learn a new language.

It is natural and understandable that you would initially be drawn to such a place and such a life; it solves many immediate problems for you. But at some point, you should consider what price you are paying for the choice you have made to live primarily in the protection of an immigrant subculture. To begin with, it means you may have very little motivation—and even less opportunity—to learn English, and *that* means you will become increasingly isolated from the wider society. As you withdraw deeper into the subculture, you cut yourself and your family off from the many opportunities and resources the majority culture can offer, settling instead for the necessarily limited opportunities available in the subculture. Even if that is good enough for you, is that what you want for your children? To always be on the outside looking in?

### 16. Try to make a gradual transition from the immigrant subculture into the mainstream culture.

You don't have to do this all at once; take your time. Some days you will spend entirely within your subculture. Then, after you've been in your new country for some time, there may be some days when you may venture outside into the English-speaking culture for short periods. And later you may spend longer and longer in the wider world.

Remember, too, that you can have the best of both worlds. Becoming a functioning member of the majority culture doesn't mean you have to turn your back on the immigrant community you once lived in. You can always participate as much as you want in that "old" life. But one thing is certain: without English you cannot become a functioning member of the majority culture.

We have offered a lot of advice here on how to improve your English. And we believe in this advice, of course; it will certainly help you if you follow it. But you have to be realistic: you don't need to be working on your English all the time or even most of the time. You just need to work on it some of the time.

There will be times when if you can just get through the

day *in your mother tongue*, you will be lucky, when the idea of improving your English is the last thing that will come into your mind. But there will be other days when things go more smoothly, good days when you are not overwhelmed by all the challenges you face. On those days, you may have the time and the energy to work on your English. The advice in this chapter is for those good days.

*Learning a native language was perhaps the best thing that ever happened to people who went out to India and those who failed to do so remained forever at a distance from the land and its people.*

—Charles Allen
*Plain Tales from the Raj*

*Every language has its own inseparable and incommunicable qualities of superiority.*

—Thomas De Quincey

# EPILOGUE: ARE YOU SERIOUS?

*It's a funny thing: the French call it a couteau, the Germans call it a messer, but we call it a knife, which is after all what it really is.*

—Richard Jenkyns
*The Victorians and Ancient Greece*

**R**eaders who've come this far could be forgiven for feeling a bit overwhelmed. "Do you actually expect us to keep 50 things in mind when we're talking to limited-English speakers?"

## Reality Check

We don't, even if you could, which is doubtful. If we have presented an admittedly comprehensive list of techniques to help you deal with immigrants and other foreigners who speak limited English, it's not because you're expected to remember and put all these suggestions into practice. It is, rather, to provide you with a complete list of all the possibilities; some you will seize upon and others you may ignore or perhaps take up at a later time.

There's a good chance, in fact, that you already practice some of these techniques, and there are several others that can be acquired with almost no effort. If you look at all 50 pieces of advice (see the collected list in Appendix A), you will see that they fall into three general categories:

- There are some techniques which most people do naturally—most people already smile and nod (#1, #2) and may slow down (#26) and not raise their voice (#27). You can take these off your list.

- There are several other techniques that you likewise do not have to think about or consciously practice because the circumstances will prompt you to do these things. When people don't understand something you say, you don't have to remind yourself to repeat what you said (#24). If people speak too fast, you will naturally ask them to slow down (#46). You will know enough to ask for help (#15) if all else fails. So you can take these off your list, too. Indeed, you should go through all 50 items in Appendix A and cross out any other suggestions you don't have to worry about, ones you feel sure the circumstances will automatically prompt you to do.

- That leaves the third category: suggestions you might have to consciously work on, that you will have to remind yourself to practice. That may still be a large group, but you don't have to start applying them all at the same time. Select one technique you think will be especially helpful to you in your job and consciously work on that one for a few weeks. After a while, it will start to become second nature. Then you can select another technique.

## Rewards

To be sure it will take effort on your part to modify some of your natural speaking habits, but if you consider for a moment the many positive results, the effort will not seem all that burdensome. To begin with, it means you will succeed in doing your job, assuming, that is, that some part of your job involves interacting with the public. Quite apart from how that may make the public feel, knowing you have fulfilled your job responsibilities will make you feel good—and make your employer feel good as well.

It also means you have enabled the people you speak with to do what they needed to do when they approached you today, to get the goods, the service, or the information—to get the *help*—they came for. That should be very satisfying for you, to say nothing of how happy it makes limited-English speakers feel.

But it does more than merely make them happy; it gives them self-confidence, the feeling that they just might be able to survive in their new country. Remember, in this context, that while this exchange with you went well, in part because you did the right things, it's only one of many encounters limited-English speakers are going to have with native speakers today, and a lot of those exchanges aren't going to go that well. Their self-confidence and self-esteem, in short, are going to take a few hits today, so how nice it must feel to have an exchange that is successful and gives them hope.

But it does more than give them hope; it gives them courage, the courage to try a few more encounters and perhaps meet a few needs they might have given up on because they knew they could never manage the language challenges. Maybe what Mr. X really needs is to apply for a driver's license, but he simply could not face the thought of standing in line at the Department of Motor Vehicles and navigating the application process. So for now he walks or takes public transportation. Then he has a successful encounter with you and thinks: maybe I can do this. Before long, Mr. X and others like him go from believing they can function in your country to feeling they can thrive, that they can contribute to and participate fully in the place they now call home. Just imagine how good that must make them feel.

There is a school of thought, incidentally, that holds that simplifying one's English when talking to limited-English speakers is a disservice, that it gives people the impression that their English is much better than it is. It might cause them to stop taking language classes, for example, or to decide they don't need to start language lessons to begin with. After all, most other native speakers aren't going to simplify *their* English, so you're just setting limited-English speakers up for disappointment.

There may be a touch of truth here, but not much. Indeed, the very fact that the typical native speaker is not going to simplify their speech will quickly disabuse limited-English speakers of any illusions they may have about their proficiency. They're not going to stop going to language class. Meanwhile, if an occasional successful interaction enhances the individual's self-image, surely someone with a positive self-image is a much better candidate for learning a new language.

At the end of the day, modifying your speech to help another person understand you is just simply a kind act. It means you have been able to put yourself in the other person's shoes and that you're thinking of them. On any given day, surely there is always room for one more act of kindness.

# APPENDIXES

# APPENDIX A

## Advice Collected

There are 50 pieces of advice scattered throughout this volume. We have collected them all here for ease of reference, along with the page number they appear on.

## Staying Calm (Chapter 4)

1. Smile. 52
2. Nod. 53
3. Don't frown. 53
4. Don't misinterpret *their* smile and *their* nod. 54
5. Don't misinterpret the meaning of "yes." 54
6. Get the person out of a line. 55
7. Create some privacy. 55
8. Reschedule the encounter. 56
9. Assure the person that you've got plenty of time. 57
10. Take the blame. 58
11. Praise their English. 58
12. Write down any words people are having trouble understanding. 59

13.  Watch their body language. 59
14.  Help them find the word or phrase they're looking for. 60
15.  Ask for help from someone who is better at this. 60

## Word Choice (Chapter 5)

16.  Don't use phrasal verbs. 62
17.  Don't use idioms. 65
18.  Use simple vocabulary. 67
19.  Become familiar with cognates; draw up a list. 69
20.  Write down words that appear difficult. 72
21.  Avoid contractions, formal and informal. 72
22.  Avoid special vocabulary: departmental, in-house, job- or profession-specific language. 76
23.  Avoid slang. 77
24.  Repeat what you said using different vocabulary. 77
25.  Use the same words *they* use. 78

## Other Speaking Habits (Chapter 6)

26.  Slow down! 82
27.  Don't raise your voice. 82
28.  Use shorter sentences. 83
29.  Use the active voice. 84
30.  Use labeling language (metadiscourse). 85
31.  Don't assume people understood you; ask them. 87
32.  Don't ask: Do you understand? Do you have any questions? 87
33.  Ask open questions. 88
34.  Assure people it's okay to have questions. 88

## Translation Frustration

## Telephone Blues (Chapter 7)

## When *You* Can't Understand *Them* (Chapter 8)

# APPENDIX B

## Test Yourself: Do I Need This Book?

1. True or False: I know what a cognate is.
2. True or False: I try to use cognates when I speak to limited-English speakers.
3. True or False: Most limited-English speakers realize I may have trouble understanding them.
4. True or False: People will tell me if they haven't understood me.
5. True or False: I know what a phrasal verb is.
6. True or False: I try not to use phrasal verbs when I speak to limited-English speakers.
7. True or False: The person may initially be nervous, but when we start talking, they will normally begin to calm down.
8. True or False: I know what an idiom is.
9. True or False: I try to avoid idioms when I speak to limited-English speakers.
10. True or False: I try to avoid contractions when I speak to limited-English speakers.

11. True or False: When people smile and nod, I know they've understood me.

12. True or False: People will ask me to repeat myself if they didn't understand something.

13. True or False: I'll know if they have understood me because I'll ask them.

14. True or False: I always slow down when speaking to a limited-English speaker.

15. True or False: I always offer to repeat myself when I am speaking to limited-English speakers.

16. True or False: Most limited-English speakers realize they speak English with an accent.

17. True or False: If people aren't looking at me, they're not paying attention.

18. Which of the following is the best way to help a limited-English speaker have a successful interaction with a public-facing employee?

    A. Make sustained eye contact.

    B. Don't show any impatience when they are speaking.

    C. Slow down when you speak.

    D. Repeatedly ask the person if they understand you.

## Diagnostic Test: Answers

1. True or False: I know what a cognate is. Circle if you answered true. See Chapter 5.

2. True or False: I try to use cognates when I speak to limited-English speakers. Circle if you answered true. See Chapter 5.

3. True or False: Most limited-English speakers realize I may have trouble understanding them. Circle if you answered false. See Chapter 3.

4. True or False: People will tell me if they haven't understood me. Circle if you answered false. See Chapter 3.

5. True or False: I know what a phrasal verb is. Circle if you answered true. See Chapter 5.

6. True or False: I try not to use phrasal verbs when I speak to limited-English speakers. Circle if you answered true. See Chapter 5.

7. True or False: The person may initially be nervous, but when we start talking, they will normally begin to calm down. Circle if you answered false. See Chapter 4.

8. True or False: I know what an idiom is. Circle if you answered true. See Chapter 5.

9. True or False: I try to avoid idioms when I speak to limited-English speakers. Circle if you answered true. See Chapter 5.

10. True or False: I try to avoid contractions when I speak to limited-English speakers. Circle if you answered true. See Chapter 5.

11. True or False: When people smile and nod, I know they've understood me. Circle if you answered false. See Chapter 4.

12. True or False: People will ask me to repeat myself if they didn't understand something. Circle if you answered false. See Chapter 3.

13. True or False: I'll know if they have understood me because I'll ask them. Circle if you answered false. See Chapter 3.

14. True or False: I always slow down when speaking to a limited-English speaker. Circle if you answered true. See Chapter 6.

15. True or False: I always offer to repeat myself when I am speaking to limited-English speakers. Circle if you answered true. See Chapter 5.

16. True or False: Most limited-English speakers realize they speak English with an accent. Circle if you answered false. See Chapter 8.

17. True or False: If people aren't looking at me, they're not paying attention. Circle if you answered false. See Chapter 9.

18. Which of the following is the best way to help a limited-English speaker have a successful interaction with an employee in a public-facing job?

    A. Make sustained eye contact.

    B. Don't show any impatience when they are speaking.

    C. Slow down when you speak.

    D. Repeatedly ask the person if they understand you.

Circle if you answered B. See Chapter 8.

## Scoring

| 12 or more correct (circled) answers: | Well done! |
| 8–11 correct answers: | Good for you |
| 6–10 correct answers: | Most people |
| 1–5 correct answers: | Keep reading |

# APPENDIX C

## Three Scenarios Debriefed

Scenario 1: You work at the reception desk in an office that offers free prenatal care to low-income pregnant women. Mrs. Garcia has come in this morning to register for the office's service, and you speak to her as follows:

| | |
|---|---|
| You: | Good morning, Mrs. Garcia. What brings you here today? |
| Mrs. Garcia: | Excuse me? |
| You: | How can I help you? |
| Mrs. Garcia: | I need your service. |
| You: | Of course. Here are some forms for you to fill out. We'll also need to verify your income. |
| Mrs. Garcia: | Yes. |
| You: | The doctor's running behind this morning, but I'll try to squeeze you in. Sorry for all the red tape, but you'll get through it. Just bring the forms back to me when you're finished. |
| Mrs. Garcia: | Yes. |

| You: | Do you have any questions? |
|---|---|
| Mrs. Garcia: | No. Thank you. |

Here are the 12 mistakes in this scenario:

1. *What brings you here* is an expression Mrs. Garcia probably doesn't know and will interpret literally, for example my car; my friend; the train.

2. *Forms* might not mean that much to her; it would be better to say *here is a paper.*

3. *Fill out* is an idiom which means *complete* or *write on.* Idioms are hard for limited-English speakers.

4. *We'll* is a contraction; it would be better to say *we will.*

5. *Verify* is a fancy word (although it has a Spanish cognate so she may know it). It might be better to say *find out* or *learn* or *determine.*

6. *Income* is likewise a bit fancy; it would be better to say *how much money you make.*

7. *Doctor's* is another contraction. This is minor but *doctor is* would be easier.

8. *Running late* is another expression. Running where? It's better to just say *late* or *behind schedule.*

9. *Squeeze you in* is another expression. *Find a time for you* is better.

10. *Red tape* is another expression without meaning. Maybe say *paperwork* or just *papers.*

11. *Get through* is an idiom; maybe say *be able to finish.*

12. *Do you have any questions?* In these circumstances, it's better not to ask a yes/no question because you probably won't

get a "no" answer even if that's the case (see Chapter 6). It's better to ask an open question such as *What questions do you have for me?*

Scenario 2: You work at the circulation desk of the local library and Mrs. Tran has come in to apply for a library card, with her two children:

| | |
|---|---|
| Mrs. Tran: | I would like to apply for a library card. |
| You: | Of course. Do you reside in the county? |
| Mrs. Tran: | Which side of the county? |
| You: | I mean. Where is your residence? |
| Mrs. Tran: | Yes, we are residents. |
| You: | Where is your house? |
| Mrs. Tran: | Oh, I see. In Rosslyn. |
| You: | Fine. Here is an application form. Please complete it and bring it back to me. |

## LATER...

| | |
|---|---|
| Mrs. Tran: | Here is my application. |
| You: | Thank you. Did you want this application to also cover your kids? |
| Mrs. Tran: | My kids? |
| You: | Yes. Your children? |
| Mrs. Tran: | Yes, please. |
| You: | You can borrow up to six books at once and two DVDs and hold on to them for three weeks. |

| Mrs. Tran: | Thank you. |
| You: | But if the books are late, there will be a fine. |
| Mrs. Tran: | It's fine if the books are late? |
| You: | No. You will have to pay. But if we are closed when you come back, there is always the book drop outside. |
| Mrs. Tran: | We can drop the books outside? |

Here are the eight mistakes:

1. *Reside* is a pretty fancy word. Just say *live*.
2. *Residence* is also fancy. Say *house*.
3. Asking Mrs. Tran to *complete* a form might be confusing. It would be easier to say *write your information on this paper*.
4. *Kids* is slang, although people learn it early on. *Children* would be better.
5. *Borrow* is library talk. Say *take home* or *take with you*.
6. *Hold on to* is probably okay but *keep* would be better.
7. *Fine* means *good*, *nice*, or *okay*. Better to say *you will have to pay some money* or maybe *a late fee*. (I'm reminded of the example often given to illustrate how difficult English can be for limited-English speakers: a sign that says *Fine for Loitering*.)
8. *Book drop* is more library talk. Say *there is a place (small door) in the wall outside* or something like that.

Scenario 3: Here's a scene in a restaurant where a limited-English couple is being waited on by their friendly server Jason. How many "difficult" things does Jason say?

| | |
|---|---|
| Jason: | Good evening. My name is Jason. I'll be your server this evening. What can I start you off with? |
| Patrons: | Excuse me? |
| Jason: | Can I get you something to drink? |
| Patrons: | Oh, yes. We'd like.... |
| Jason: | Sure. Let me grab those for you while you look over the menu. |

**LATER...**

| | |
|---|---|
| Jason: | So, here are your drinks. We have several specials tonight. Can I go over them for you? |
| Patrons: | Yes, it's a very special night. |
| Jason: | No, I mean some dishes that are not on the menu. |
| Patrons: | Oh, then we can't have those tonight? |
| Jason: | No, I mean they're not written on the menu. |
| Patrons: | Oh, of course. |

**(JASON DESCRIBES THE SPECIALS.)**

| | |
|---|---|
| Jason: | I'll give you a few minutes. |

**LATER...**

| | |
|---|---|
| Jason: | So, have we made up our minds? |
| Patrons: | Excuse me? |
| Jason: | I mean can I take your orders? |
| Patrons: | Our orders? |

Here are the eight mistakes:

1. *Server* is nonstandard; Jason should just say *waiter.*
2. *Start you off* is idiomatic; he should say *what would you like to drink?*
3. Avoid *grab* and say *get* or *bring* instead.
4. Avoid *look over* and say *look at* instead.
5. Instead of just saying *specials*, say *some special dishes (choices) that are not on the menu but we are offering tonight.*
6. Rather than saying *give you a few minutes*, maybe say *take your time to look at the menu and I'll come back.*
7. *Made up your mind* is an expression. It's better to use *have you decided?*
8. Avoid *orders* and say *choices* or *selections* instead.

You might quibble about a few of these "mistakes"—some of them are rather elementary, even for those with limited English. But you get the point.

# APPENDIX D

## Phrasal Verbs

1. back down     to decide not to do something because of opposition
2. back out of     to decide not to follow through on or complete something
3. back up     to support with evidence or proof
4. break up     to end a relationship
5. bring about     to cause something to happen
6. bring up     to raise a matter for discussion
7. call off     to cancel a planned event
8. call on     to visit
9. chip in     to contribute
10. come down with     to become ill with
11. count on     to rely or depend on
12. cut back     to reduce
13. cut off     to stop the supply of
14. die down/die away     to become less, diminish
15. do away with     to get rid of, eliminate
16. do over     to do again, repeat
17. drop by/drop in     to visit

| | |
|---|---|
| 18. figure out | to come to understand, to find the answer or solution |
| 19. fill in | to inform |
| 20. fill out | to write information down in the blanks of a form (the British say fill *in*) |
| 21. find out | to learn or discover |
| 22. get along | to like or be friendly with |
| 23. get over | to recover from (an illness, a shock) |
| 24. give up | to stop trying to do something that's too hard |
| 25. go over | to review, study closely |
| 26. hold on | to wait for a short time |
| 27. iron out | to resolve a problem or differences |
| 28. keep at | to continue |
| 29. keep from | to hide or not divulge |
| 30. look after | to take care of |
| 31. look down on | to consider yourself superior to someone else |
| 32. look into | to investigate |
| 33. look up to | to admire |
| 34. look out | be careful |
| 35. make up with | to become friends after an argument |
| 36. mess up | to do something poorly or wrong |
| 37. own up to | to admit to |
| 38. pass away | to die |
| 39. pass out | to lose consciousness or faint |
| 40. pass up | to forgo, do without |
| 41. pick on | to criticize or tease |
| 42. piss off | to annoy |

| 43. | play down | to de-emphasize the importance of something |
| 44. | pull off | to succeed in doing something difficult |
| 45. | put off | to postpone or move to a later time |
| 46. | put out | to extinguish |
| 47. | put up with | to tolerate |
| 48. | run into | to meet someone by chance |
| 49. | run out of | to not have any more of |
| 50. | see about | to arrange or organize something |
| 51. | see to | to take care of, look after, be responsible for |
| 52. | show up | to arrive at an event or appointment |
| 53. | sit back | to do nothing, make no effort |
| 54. | speak up | to talk louder |
| 55. | stick to | to not quit or not stop |
| 56. | talk out of | to change someone's mind |
| 57. | tell off | to strongly criticize someone |
| 58. | turn down | to refuse or not agree to a request |
| 59. | use up | to not have any left |
| 60. | watch out | be careful |

# APPENDIX E

## Idioms

1. hit the nail on the head — to say something exactly right
2. take it easy — to relax, calm down
3. piece of cake — easy or simple
4. the last straw — the final problem in a long series
5. under the weather — to feel ill, sick, not well
6. miss the boat — to miss one's chance or opportunity
7. all ears — listening, eager
8. see eye to eye — when two people agree on something
9. an arm and a leg — a very high price for a product or service
10. sit on the fence — to remain neutral, having no opinion
11. up in the air — unresolved, undecided, not certain
12. a far cry from — completely different from
13. take something with a grain of salt — to not take something seriously

| | | |
|---|---|---|
| 14. | a penny for your thoughts | inquiring about the thoughts or feelings of someone else |
| 15. | a short fuse | quick to anger |
| 16. | a stone's throw | very close, a short distance |
| 17. | out on a limb | taking a chance, taking a risk |
| 18. | add insult to injury | to make a bad situation worse |
| 19. | method to my madness | there is a reason for seemingly irrational or arbitrary behavior |
| 20. | at the drop of a hat | without any hesitation |
| 21. | back to the drawing board | to start over after an unsuccessful attempt |
| 22. | barking up the wrong tree | doing or pursuing something wrong |
| 23. | the ball is in your court | it's your decision |
| 24. | beat around the bush | to delay or avoid talking about something difficult or unpleasant |
| 25. | bend over backward | to make a great effort |
| 26. | best of both worlds | having many advantages |
| 27. | best thing since sliced bread | a very good idea, plan, or innovation |
| 28. | bite off more than you can chew | to try to do too much |
| 29. | love is blind | unable to see faults in a person you love |
| 30. | not (someone's) cup of tea | of no interest to someone |
| 31. | blow off steam | to talk loudly in a way that displays anger |
| 32. | bread and butter | something central or fundamental |

| | | |
|---|---|---|
| 33. | make a long story short | to come to the point, leave out details |
| 34. | bring home the bacon | to earn money through a job |
| 35. | burn the midnight oil | to work hard and late into the night |
| 36. | call it a day | to declare the day's work finished |
| 37. | don't judge a book by its cover | to judge only by external appearances |
| 38. | give the benefit of the doubt | to believe someone's statement without proof |
| 39. | cat's got someone's tongue | someone is speechless |
| 40. | chin up | be happy, cheer up |
| 41. | cross that bridge when you come to it | to deal with something only when it arises, becomes necessary |
| 42. | cry over spilled milk | to worry about an unfortunate event that has already occurred |
| 43. | cry wolf | to call for help when you don't need it |
| 44. | wouldn't be caught dead | would never even consider doing something |
| 45. | cut corners | to take shortcuts, do something poorly |
| 46. | at the drop of a hat | instantly, without hesitation |
| 47. | cut to the chase | to get to the point |
| 48. | don't put all your eggs in one basket | don't dedicate all your energy or resources to just one thing |
| 49. | draw the line | to set a limit or boundary |
| 50. | drive someone up the wall | to make someone very angry or annoyed |

51. keep something at bay — to keep something away
52. in the heat of the moment — overwhelmed by something that has just happened
53. devil's advocate — to present a counter argument
54. a blessing in disguise — something good that is not recognized at first
55. a hot potato — a controversial issue everyone is talking about
56. to scratch someone's back — to help/do a favor for someone in hopes the person will return the favor
57. to lose your touch — to lose a talent you once possessed
58. sit tight — to be patient and not act immediately on something
59. on the ball — quick to understand, notice or act on something
60. take it easy — relax

# APPENDIX F

## Common American Slang

Limited-English speakers may recognize many of these words, but they will not know the slang meaning. And neither will some Brits!

|    |            |                                                      |
|----|------------|------------------------------------------------------|
| 1. | cool       | great, fantastic, very nice                          |
| 2. | a lemon    | something that is broken or does not work as it is supposed to |
| 3. | a buck     | one dollar                                           |
| 4. | cop        | police officer                                       |
| 5. | chicken    | coward, cowardly                                     |
| 6. | drunk      | intoxicated                                          |
| 7. | booze      | alcohol                                              |
| 8. | pig out    | to overeat, eat too much                             |
| 9. | beat       | tired                                                |
| 10.| dough      | money                                                |
| 11.| no big deal| not important, not serious                          |
| 12.| in no time | very quickly                                         |
| 13.| What's up? | How are you?                                         |
| 14.| I get it   | I understand                                         |

15. same here        I agree
16. you bet          sure, fine, OK
17. no sweat         not difficult, easy
18. to be fired      to lose your job
19. a blast          a lot of fun
20. show up          to come, to arrive
21. screw up         to make a mistake, do something the wrong way
22. wrap up          to conclude, bring to an end
23. make waves       cause trouble
24. neat             good, similar to cool above
25. nuts             crazy
26. riot             very funny

# APPENDIX G

## Common British Slang

Limited-English speakers will not know the meaning of many of these words—and neither will a lot of Americans!

| | | |
|---|---|---|
| 1. | bloke | a guy or man |
| 2. | bloody | very |
| 3. | bonkers | crazy |
| 4. | cheeky | a little rude |
| 5. | cheers | thanks |
| 6. | chuffed | very pleased or happy |
| 7. | cock-up | a mistake |
| 8. | cuppa | a cup of tea |
| 9. | daft | silly, foolish, nonsense |
| 10. | dim | not intelligent |
| 11. | doddle | an easy task, not difficult |
| 12. | dodgy | suspicious, questionable |
| 13. | quid | a British pound (monetary) |
| 14. | fancy | to desire or want |
| 15. | fiver | a five-pound note |
| 16. | flog | to sell cheaply |

| 17. | knackered | very tired, exhausted |
| 18. | loo | toilet |
| 19. | mate | friend |
| 20. | miffed | annoyed, upset |
| 21. | mug | face |
| 22. | nick | to steal |
| 23. | pinch | to steal |
| 24. | plastered | drunk |
| 25. | rank | unpleasant |
| 26. | rubbish | absurd, nonsense |
| 27. | super | excellent, first class |
| 28. | ta | thanks (thank you) |
| 29. | tenner | a 10-pound note |
| 30. | whinge/whinger | to complain (a complainer) |

# APPENDIX H

## English-Spanish Cognates

| | | | |
|---|---|---|---|
| accident | accidente | hour | hora |
| activities | activadades | human | humano |
| adult | adulto | idea | idea |
| agent | agente | identification | identificación |
| artist | artista | information | información |
| attention | atención | inspection | inspección |
| cabin | cabina | intelligence | inteligencia |
| center | centro | invitation | invitación |
| class | clase | lemon | limón |
| coast | costa | lesson | lección |
| company | compañía | line | linea |
| directions | direcciones | list | lista |
| distance | distancia | manner | manera |
| factor | factor | map | mapa |
| family | familia | million | millón |
| fruit | fruta | minute | minuto |
| group | grupo | moment | momento |
| history | historia | music | música |
| hospital | hospital | object | objeto |

| | | | |
|---|---|---|---|
| occasion | ocasión | plant | planta |
| park | parque | problem | problema |
| part | parte | television | televisión |
| patience | paciencia | tourist | turista |
| photo | foto | traffic | tráfico |
| plans | planes | vegetables | vegetales |

# APPENDIX I

## English-Spanish false friends

When a native speaker uses the English word, a Spanish speaker will attach the Spanish meaning. When a Spanish speaker uses the Spanish word, a native speaker will attach the English meaning. Both speakers will be making a mistake.

| English word | Spanish "friend" | Meaning in Spanish |
|---|---|---|
| 1. exit | éxito | success |
| 2. bigot | bigote | moustache |
| 3. camp | campo | countryside |
| 4. cart | carta | letter |
| 5. compromise | compromiso | commitment |
| 6. conference | conferencia | lecture |
| 7. constipated | constipado | cold |
| 8. contest | contestar | to answer |
| 9. embarrassed | embarazada | pregnant |
| 10. envy | enviar | to send |

| 11. eventually | eventualmente | by chance, occasionally |
|---|---|---|
| 12. grab | grabar | to record |
| 13. impression | impresionar | to shock |
| 14. inconsequential | inconsecuente | inconsistent |
| 15. introduce | introducir | to insert |
| 16. molest | molestar | to annoy |
| 17. present | presentar | to introduce |
| 18. preservative | preservativo | condom |
| 19. pretend | pretender | to intend or to woo |
| 20. profound | profundo | exhaustive, detailed |
| 21. rapist | rapista | barber |
| 22. realize | realizar | to carry out or achieve |
| 23. record | recordar | to remember |
| 24. support | soportar | to put up with |
| 25. ultimately | ultimamente | recently |

# APPENDIX J

## Common Contractions

Contractions leave out entire syllables; limited-English speakers may not know what has been left out. The most common contractions involve a helping or auxiliary verb, of which the most common are:

1. is (the verb *to be*)
2. have
3. will
4. would

|  | **Contraction** | **Negative form** |
|---|---|---|
| **1. to be:** | I'm | I'm not |
|  | you're | you're not/you aren't |
|  | he's/she's/it's | he/she/it isn't |
|  | we're | we're not/we aren't |
|  | you're | you're not/you aren't |
|  | they're | they're not/they aren't |

The verb *to be* in the third person—the word *is*—is often changed to the letter *s* and added to many different words:

What's (What is) the problem?    The baby's (baby is) sick.
That's (That is) interesting.    There's (There is) no time.

**2. have**        I've                    I haven't
                   you've                  you haven't
                   he's/she's/it's         he/she/it hasn't
                   we've                   we haven't
                   you've                  you haven't
                   they've                 they haven't

**3. will**        I'll                    I won't
                   you'll                  you won't
                   he'll/she'll/it'll      he/she/it won't
                   we'll                   we won't
                   you'll                  you won't
                   they'll                 they won't

**4. would**       I'd                     I wouldn't
                   you'd                   you wouldn't
                   he'd/she'd/it'd         he/she/it wouldn't
                   we'd                    we wouldn't
                   you'd                   you wouldn't
                   they'd                  they wouldn't

**would have/should have**      I would've/should've
                                you would've/should've
                                he/she/it would've/should've
                                we would've/should've
                                you would've/should've
                                they would've/should've

# APPENDIX K

## Common Indian English Words

When Indians use these words, you will apply the native speaker meaning. When you use these words, Indians will apply the Indian English meaning. Both of you will assume you understand and that you have been understood. And you'll both be wrong.

| Word or expression | Meaning in US English | Meaning in Indian English |
|---|---|---|
| 1. bouncer | a nightclub doorman | something not understood: *That was a total bouncer.* |
| 2. cabin | a small hut or dwelling | an office or cubicle |
| 3. clubbing | beating or going to nightclubs | joining or combining something together |
| 4. coach | a train car or an athletic guide | a bus |
| 5. curd | a soft, white substance used as the basis of cheese | yogurt |
| 6. doubt, as in *I have a doubt*. | disbelief | a question |
| 7. excuse, as in *Thank you for your excuse*. | an attempt to be forgiven | reason or logic |
| 8. flyover | something jets do | an overpass |
| 9. fresher | the comparative form of *fresh* | a new hire, rookie |
| 10. homely | unattractive in appearance | Adjective: a good cook, homemaker, housewife |
| 11. intimate (verb) | suggest or imply | inform or notify |
| 12. jumper | a person who jumps | a sweater |
| 13. mad | angry or upset | crazy |
| 14. mail | letters, etc. | electronic mail |
| 15. out of station | NA | not in the office, out of town |

| | | |
|---|---|---|
| 16. pass out/a passout | faint or become unconscious | graduate or complete your studies/a graduate |
| 17. post | a stick in the ground | regular mail |
| 18. prepone | NA | move forward, do sooner |
| 19. purse (noun) | a woman's handbag | a wallet |
| 20. return ticket | the return portion of a round-trip ticket | a round-trip ticket |
| 21. revert | return to an earlier way of doing something, go back to | reply or respond (as to an email) |
| 22. rubber | condom, latex material | an eraser |
| 23. smart, as in *You look smart.* | intelligent | well-dressed, dapper |
| 24. snaps | NA | photos |
| 25. STD | sexually transmitted disease | single trunk dial (long-distance phone call inside India) |
| 26. tick off | annoy | check off, mark as complete |
| 27. throw up | vomit | uncover or reveal |
| 28. too easy | suspiciously easy | very easy |
| 29. too good | suspiciously good | very good |
| 30. vest | sleeveless jacket | undershirt |

A number of these words are also British English.

# ENDNOTES

Chapter 1

1. Lynne Murphy, *The Prodigal Tongue: The Love-Hate Relationship between American and British English* (London: Penguin, 2018), 296.
2. "Ranking Tables," Census.gov, United States Census Bureau, February 24, 2022, https://www.census.gov/acs/www/data/data-tables-and-tools/ranking-tables/.
3. Budiman, Abby, "Key Findings about U.S. Immigrants," Pew Research Center, September 22, 2020, https://www.pewresearch.org/fact-tank/2020/08/20/key-findings-about-u-s-immigrants/.
4. "English Language Use and Proficiency of Migrants in the UK," The Migration Observatory, July 17, 2019, https://migrationobservatory.ox.ac.uk/resources/briefings/english-language-use-and-proficiency-of-migrants-in-the-uk/.
5. Keung, Nicholas, "Lost for Words: One in Every 20 Torontonians Can't Speak English or French, Study Finds," *Toronto Star*, July 8, 2018, https://www.thestar.com/news/gta/2018/07/08/lost-for-words-one-in-every-20-torontonians-cant-speak-english-or-french-study-finds.html.
6. "Proficiency in English," .id (informed decisions) for Australia, Australian Bureau of Statistics, Census of Population and Housing (2011 and 2016), https://profile.id.com.au/australia/speaks-english.
7. Moritz Thomsen, *Living Poor: An American's Encounter with Ecuador* (London: Eland, 1989), 23–24.

Chapter 2

1. Freya Stark, *The Journey's Echo: Selected Travel Writings* (New York: Ecco Press, 1988), 4.

2. Jie Zong, Jeanne Batalova Jie Zong and Jeanne Batalova, "The Limited English Proficient Population in the United States in 2013." *Migration Policy Institute*, July 20, 2020, https://www.migrationpolicy.org/article/limited-english-proficient-population-united-states-2013#:~:text=As%20of%202013%2C%20the%20highest,%2C%20Illinois%20(1.1%20million%2C%204.

Chapter 3

1. Murphy, 134.
2. "Latin American," University of San Diego, ESL and Cultures Resource, https://sites.sandiego.edu/esl/latin-american.

Chapter 9

1. Engholm, Christopher, *When Business East Meets Business West* (New York: John Wiley & Sons, 1991) 134-35.
2. "Mehrabian's 7-38-55 Communication Model: It's More than Words." *The World of Work Project*, July 26, 2021, https://worldofwork.io/2019/07/mehrabians-7-38-55-communication-model/.

Chapter 10

1. Badrinathan, Sumitra, Devesh Kapur, Jonathan Kay, and Milan Vaishnav, "Social Realities of Indian Americans: Results from the 2020 Indian American Attitudes Survey," Carnegie Endowment for International Peace, June 9, 2021, https://carnegieendowment.org/2021/06/09/social-realities-of-indian-americans-results-from-2020-indian-american-attitudes-survey-pub-84667.
2. "Indian Population in United Kingdom 2021," Find Easy, September 27, 2021, https://www.findeasy.in/indian-population-in-united-kingdom/.
3. Anderson, Stuart, "Indians Immigrating to Canada at an Astonishing Rate," Forbes, *Forbes Magazine*, December 10, 2021, https://www.forbes.com/sites/stuartanderson/2020/02/03/indians-immigrating-to-canada-at-an-astonishing-rate/?sh=ad1d74a2b5f2.
4. "Indian Population in Australia 2021," Australian Bureau of Statistics (2020), Find Easy, September 26, 2021, https://www.findeasy.in/indian-population-in-australia/.

# INDEX